Blockbuster TV

Must-See Sitcoms in the Network Era

JANET STAIGER

NEW YORK UNIVERSITY PRESS

New York and London

NEW YORK UNIVERSITY PRESS
New York and London

Library of Congress Cataloging-in-Publication Data
Staiger, Janet.
Blockbuster TV : must-see sitcoms in the network era /
Janet Staiger.
p.   cm.
Includes bibliographical references and index.
ISBN 0-8147-9756-3 (cloth : acid-free paper) —
ISBN 0-8147-9757-1 (paper : acid-free paper)
1. Television comedies—United States—History and criticism.
I. Title.
PN1992.8.C66 S718 2000
791.45'617—dc21   00-009853

New York University Press books are printed on acid-free paper,
and their binding materials are chosen for strength and durability.

Manufactured in the United States of America

10 9 8 7 6 5 4 3 2 1

To JoAnn, Don, and Diane,
   in delighted memory of our childhood

Contents

Preface

This little book isn't meant to be anything like a full picture of the television industry, American broadcasting audiences, or the events around the four situation comedies studied. Rather it is designed to be provocative—a gesture toward thinking about and researching the public reception of TV programs in relation to the institutional dynamics of network-era television.

The process of writing this book has been somewhat eye-opening. As I shall discuss in chapter 1, I am considering four *blockbuster* sitcoms, defined as a series program that achieved audience ratings markedly higher than those of any of its contenders, week after week, after 1960 (usually the date selected as the time by which almost every U.S. household had a television set and enough stations operated to provide adequate competition for audiences). The programs that meet these criteria are *The Beverly Hillbillies*, *All in the Family*, *Laverne & Shirley* (with *Happy Days*), and *The Cosby Show*.

While doing this research, I enjoyed presenting these criteria to academic colleagues and asking them to guess which programs fit this definition. Invariably, their first answers included *The Mary Tyler Moore Show*, *M*A*S*H*, *Roseanne*, and *Seinfeld*. Although very popular programs, none of these sitcoms fits this definition of a blockbuster. What these programs do coordinate with is, likely, academic taste preferences. I spend a great deal of effort (and some charts) in chapter 1 exploring what exactly were the

TV audience's preferences. This effort may seem excessive to some, but for me it is very important—in large part to dispel an impression of the history of television that is perhaps colored by class tastes and cultural capital. What this book considers is what the largest audiences found worth watching each week, not what academics enjoy or nostalgically imagine or hope were the people's tastes. (In fact, I do not particularly personally enjoy three of the four programs studied, although my research has led me to appreciate them more.)

I focus on situation comedies because of the genre's repeated ability to produce blockbuster hits for network broadcasting. While I shall point out that no single theory of comedy or culture explains this genre's appeal, I did not expect that result going into the project. Looking back at it now, I perhaps should have also studied *Dallas* as I have examined these series. It does rate as a blockbuster, and it did generate numerous imitators. It might also be considered, vaguely, a comedy. With a little less facetiousness, however, I do admit that had I been examining all blockbusters, then *Dallas* (and *Bonanza*, although it is the end of a cycle) would have been in the group. However, *Dallas* is a unique event, and it appears that melodramas do not have the consistent ability to generate blockbuster viewing and network turnarounds. I do hope that others will follow up on the model of study presented here and apply it to other programs.[1]

Thus, one eye-opening consequence of the research was not to trust one's own taste preferences when projecting back on TV history. A second one is how much work needs to be done to integrate the study of the history of U.S. broadcasting and that of its sibling, film. Significant differences do exist between the two media—some differences constructed arbitrarily by federal regulation and intervention. However, it no longer suffices for us to treat these media as existing in isolation from each other.

Readers may question why I turn to events in the history of film or to speculations about spectatorship produced as part of cinematic research for answers about television. The reasons are several: For one thing, film scholarship occasionally has had insights useful to television research, and vice versa. Additionally, comparing the two media may help us better see similarities and differences. However, most importantly, to dissociate the media is to put blinders on the history of U.S. media and culture. Two excellent examples of avoiding this territorialism and border construction are Michele Hilmes's *Hollywood and Broadcasting* and Chris Anderson's *Hollywood TV*.[2]

This work is part of my continuing interest in how to write contextual studies of the production and reception of media. Here I am providing some thoughts about one question in television studies: How can we account for the blockbuster hit? What factors might be the contextual horizons necessary for answering such a question? This work goes back to at least my doctoral research on the Hollywood mode of production and to my more recent scholarship on audience interpretation. While this is my first explicit publication in the area of television, it is the consequence of some twenty years of work on modern media.

*　　*　　*

This specific project started in the fall of 1991 while I was auditing a course in the history of broadcasting taught by my colleague Thomas Schatz. It produced conversations between us during the spring of 1992, and we jointly authored a paper on *The Beverly Hillbillies* presented at the Console-ing Passions conference in April 1993. Although my further research has deviated from our presentation there, I am indebted to Tom for our early collaborative work. Also to be thanked are the students in my graduate class on the TV sitcom (fall 1993), many graduate students whose work on television enriched my understanding of the medium, three student researchers—Eric Schaefer, Dan Streible, and Alisa Perren—and my other TV colleague, Horace Newcomb, who has also encouraged my interest and suggested programs worth viewing week after week. Besides the 1993 Console-ing Passions audience, I appreciate the feedback from the 1996 Console-ing Passions audience as well.

Several archives and archivists deserve special thanks: Academy of Motion Picture Arts and Sciences Library and Scott Curtis; Broadcast Pioneers Library of American Broadcasting; Michael Mashon; the Library of Congress; the Museum of Television and Radio; the New York Public Library; the University of California at Los Angeles Libraries and Archives; and the University of Southern California Archives. Significant appreciation goes to the University of Texas at Austin Faculty Research Assignment program which permitted me time to devote to this work.

This book is dedicated to my siblings—JoAnn Voelte Washa, Don Voelte, Jr., and Diane Voelte Fields. As the oldest child in our family, I may be the only one who remembers when Dad and Mom brought home our first TV in the middle of the FCC freeze. We had two stations in Omaha—a CBS affiliate on channel 6 and NBC on channel 3. I recall the furor over the projected addition of channel 7 (ABC): the stations would interfere with each other! My sense of national and world history is mediated by that TV. I vaguely recall the Mc-Carthy congressional hearings and the coronation of Queen Elizabeth II. At least I think I do. However, most of all, I remember how the two central objects in our household, what physically meant "family," were the kitchen table and the TV. We debated, laughed, and held our breaths together because of what television brought into our home. It has without a doubt made us what we all are today. With that loving and hopeful memory, I dedicate this book to you.

[1]
Introduction

Sigmund Freud writes at the beginning of *Jokes and Their Relation to the Unconscious* that two reasons exist to study humor. One is "an intimate connection between all mental happenings."[1] The other: "A new joke acts almost like an event of universal interest; it is passed from one person to another like the news of the latest victory" (p. 15). Two notions are important in this latter reason—"person to person" and "news of the latest victory." In studying the history of culture, history (as well as culture) must be explained. The processes of social interaction and change are important. Thus, as Freud and many others note, descriptions and explanations of the circulation of cultural discourses are worth studying.

For example, popular knowledges and social life are filled with materials from entertainment media. In the area I will be examining—several television sitcoms—I could turn to a most recent example, *Seinfeld*. This program has popularized many catchphrases such as "soup Nazi," "double-dipper," the "yada-yada-yada" conversation filler, the euphemism "master of his domain," and others. Even if one doesn't watch the program, it is difficult to evade *Seinfeld*'s discursive impact.

Figuring out why some programs and movies produce a widespread cultural awareness of their fictional worlds would be a great achievement, but an impossible one. However, describing parts of the processes by which some television programs became extremely noteworthy is at least a contribution toward this broader research question. My focus in this book is, Can we explain the phenomenon of the unusually popular TV sitcom within the contexts of American entertainment media?

One of the most powerful sites for both discourse creation and discourse circulation is the American television situation comedy. In the medium of television, the sitcom has proven to be the most popular genre. Year after year, sitcoms appear in the top-ten ratings. Network executives and television critics have attempted to explain this. Among the answers suggested have been that the half-hour format fits the audience's attention span; situation comedies can reflect rapidly the interests of the contemporary audience; and the humor of sitcoms flatters viewers who feel superior to the sitcom characters or identify with their plights. These and other suggested answers I will review below, but while all of these explanations are likely part of the story, none of them—or even all of them together—can quite explain a second phenomenon about TV sitcoms. In the history of American television, breakaway hits in the ratings are most likely to be sitcoms. By the term "breakaway hits" I mean that the ratings for the shows significantly exceed those of their second- or third-rated (or even lower) competitors; the programs are "ratings busters" or in Hollywood movie terms "blockbusters." These programs are constituted somehow as more than routine programs.

"Least objectionable programming" (LOP) is an industry theory about why people pick what they want to see—when they want to watch TV, they choose the LOP channel. This hypothesis about viewers probably covers a great deal of the time they spend with the TV. However, the blockbuster phenomenon suggests something more than LOP is occurring. Ratings-busting programs are garnering audience attention beyond normal viewing behaviors, evidenced by the disparity between their ratings numbers and those of the average success. We are familiar with individual instances of such audience focus—the season opening for the "Who Shot J.R.?" episode of *Dallas*, the miniseries *Roots*, the final show for *M*A*S*H*, the annual Superbowl game. These and other individual television moments become American mass events, authenticating the metaphors of television as a national hearth or a global village.

Thus, studying how a program, or in this case four sitcoms, could weekly achieve the repeated semblance of this group experience and focus is important for understanding how mass media institutions and American audiences interrelate. The four blockbuster programs are *The Beverly Hillbillies*, *All in the Family*, *Laverne & Shirley* (with *Happy Days*), and *The Cosby Show*. While the theoretical and critical explanations often provided for the popularity of sitcoms can account for the wide appeal of the shows, it is necessary to add historical and institutional factors to understand the ratings buster.[2]

For one thing, diverse public institutional systems stimulate the broadening, or even the focusing, of audiences. "Surrogate consumers," spokespersons for these public institutions, praise or challenge these hit programs for various reasons, bringing in different subaudiences to view the sitcom.[3] Surrogate consumers most obviously are critics, assigned to give the public an idea of what might be in the product were they to choose it, but any public commentator might become a surrogate consumer. In criticizing *Murphy Brown* for supposedly parading a single mother as a model, Dan Quayle functioned as a surrogate consumer.

Obviously, some surrogate consumers reach many more potential customers than do other surrogate consumers; some critics are much more influential than others. Yet almost any notice, even by individuals not considered to have the same tastes as the subaudience, can produce an awareness of a program. As the saying goes, no publicity is bad publicity. The consequences of public awareness of the hit can be the "must-see-TV" syndrome, propelled in part by desires for social community and cultural currency. Then familiarity breeds interest and repeated consumption.

This sequence does not always work in such a top-down matter. With literature, theater, film, music, and television, at times surrogate consumers find themselves struggling to explain the popularity of a text, song, or program that gathers audiences for reasons the surrogate consumers consider unfathomable. In these cases, the explanations for the unusual success have to be drawn from other factors. Yet even the public accounting for the disjunction between the surrogate consumers' opinions and many customers' views increases the visibility of the show.

For either case—programs developed as a result of significant public discourse or programs "spontaneously" drawing in large numbers of viewers—the period of convergence is brief. Although often written to the same formula, the series' days of celebrity are fleeting, usually three to four years. While the programs may linger on the air, they peak and then drop into LOP levels. New thrills replace them or the public is fickle, moving on in its interests and tastes.

What is noticed about these programs by their surrogate consumers or the mass audience differs from case to case, and the composition of the audience reached changes as well. Thus, the particular histories of the ratings busters are distinct although the institutional processes are similar. These processes are not unknown to the networks and their publicists, but what works is highly unpredictable. Even good word of mouth from surrogate consumers can't insure the attention of subgroups. NBC can label its recent successful Thursday night lineups as "must-see-TV," but it cannot force people to turn on the TV or tune in its affiliate channel. Hence, I will not be able to supply any magical formulas to produce a new blockbuster but can only trace what happened previously.

I May Not Know If It's a Sitcom, But I Know What I Like

The notion of "situation comedy" likely requires little explication given its common use. In fact, trying to define it would be very difficult. As soon as one set of terms is applied, exceptions are obvious. For example, Gerard Jones suggests the network situation comedy is typified by the formula of *The Cosby Show:*

Domestic harmony is threatened when a character develops a desire that runs counter to the group's welfare, or misunderstands a situation because of poor communication, or contacts a disruptive outside element. The voice of the group—usually the voice of the father or equivalent chief executive—tries to restore harmony but fails. The dissenter grabs at an easy, often unilateral solution. The solution fails, and the dissenter must surrender to the group for rescue. The problem turns out to be not very serious after all, once everyone remembers to communicate and surrender his or her selfish goals. The wisdom of the group and its executive is proved. Everyone, including the dissenter, is happier than at the outset.[4]

This description does work for *The Cosby Show*, but Jones then has to backtrack almost immediately in his discussion of *I Love Lucy*, where the resolution is "authoritarian" (p. 80).

The same problem occurs when distinctions among types of comic formulas are attempted. The purpose of Horace Newcomb's *TV: The Most Popular Art* is to define the prevalent TV genres through a neo-Aristotelian critical method of describing their setting, situation, characters, and values. Newcomb distinguishes between the situation comedy and the domestic comedy. On the one hand, the situation comedy is determined primarily by the narrative complication: the central character takes an "improbable" response to a situation that produces confusion until it is resolved.[5] On the other hand, the domestic comedy has "a richer variety of event, a consequent deepening of character, and a sense of seriousness" (p. 43). It is set in the home and its environments, with strong gender typing for the parents. The event produces a learning process, with the family as a "sheltering unit" (p. 55). Yet, for *The Mary Tyler Moore Show*, Jane Feuer argues that "the situation itself becomes a pretext for the revelation of character"[6]—creating a plot formula that Newcomb has assigned to the domestic comedy. A response to this apparent contradiction in definitions might be to point out how the workplace in *The Mary Tyler Moore Show* has become the family home, placing the program in the domestic comedy arena. Yet it is still the situation rather than a "richer event" that precipitates the humor.

The point is that as soon as one tries to define situation comedy or domestic comedy, or warmedy or dramedy, exceptions can be noted. Moreover, these terms and the formulas and complications of situation comedies have a history in radio and film prior to their applications in television. For example, in 1946, in a discussion of what would work on the fledgling new medium, broadcast commentator John F. Royal predicted that "television comedy will be the key to the success of video."[7] Moreover, presciently he indicated that the comedy would not be gag comedy but "the legitimate or situation-and-plot format" (p. 1).

The notion of "domestic comedy" was also already well established within radio and the movie industry before the beginnings of commercial television. In a listing of proposed films for the 1939–40 season, the following movies were labeled "domestic comedy": three to-be-titled "Blondies" from the newspaper comic strip for Columbia; "I Love You Again" (MGM); untitled "Hardy Families" and "American Newlyweds" (also MGM); and Twentieth-Century Fox's "The Jones Family."[8]

Thus, for the purposes of the discussion here, I intend to use the term situation comedy (and sitcom) as self-evident and rather all-encompassing. While I will be discussing how public discourse perceived features of the programs and sometimes marked them out as innovative, I shall not try to define narrowly or exclusively the constituents of the genre. Moreover, although I would not go so far as to claim with Newcomb that "it is even possible to say that the television mystery or Western is more comparable to the television situation comedy than to the literary forms of either of those two standard formulas" (p. 23), I do believe along with him that the success of the situation comedy has inflected all other television programs. The function of multiple plotlines in film and radio narratives, and now in television, has been to broaden the affective dynamics available to the audience, encouraging pleasure in at least one if not all of the causal chains.[9] The very pervasiveness of comedy, humor, and joking in TV is symptomatic of one of the most obvious reasons we watch it: for entertainment. It would be a mistake to try to essentialize its causes, its formulas, and its receptions.[10]

Moreover, as I shall discuss, the four blockbuster sitcoms each turn on very different types of "comedy." Responses to *The Beverly Hillbillies* suggest that the general audience may have been enjoying the puns and malapropisms, while a high-brow audience saw the program as satire. *All in the Family* used sarcasm to a great extent as its comedic ploy. *Laverne & Shirley* employed slapstick and situational comedy. *The Cosby Show* worked mostly in the realm of humor. Thus, I shall also not attempt to marshal up one or two theories of comedy, humor, and joking in an attempt to account for some underlying cultural dynamic. Too much variation exists to homogenize these very different programs and experiences.[11]

"Demography Democracy"

One way to calculate what counts as a blockbuster, as must-see-TV, is to consider programs for which ratings exceed in some rather demonstrative way the numbers for competitors.[12] Thus, chart 1 notes the ratings for the top three programs for the period of 1950 to the present. Although some programs in the 1950s achieved spectacular ratings, it was not until the late 1950s that television sets were firmly ensconced in a reasonably full penetration of U.S. households and most viewing areas had at least two and possibly three network affiliate channels providing reasonable competition for the audiences.[13] Since I am interested in the mass phenomenon of viewing, it seems appropriate to start the observations at this point, 1960. Thus, I have three criteria for blockbusters: (1) the series secures audience ratings that are significantly higher than those of its nearest competitors; (2) it secures these ratings week after week (for at least one year); and (3) it begins after 1960, when audience ratings basically represent a competitive and national U.S. television population.[14]

Within the history of prime-time TV, seven programs (including a strong duo) secured ratings that were significantly higher than the second- or third-place programs, suggesting people were doing something more than their normal TV watching. In other words, the numbers were high enough to

CHART 1

Top Three Programs, 1950–

Date/ Rating	Difference	Program	Network	Time Slot	Notes
1950–51					
61.6		Texaco Star Theater	NBC	T 8:00	
52.6		Fireside Theater	NBC	T 9:00	
45.3		Philco TV Playhouse	NBC	Su 9:00	
1951–52					
53.8		Arthur Godfrey	CBS	M 8:30	
52.0		Texaco Star Theater	NBC	T 8:00	
50.9		I Love Lucy	CBS	M 9:00	first year hits top 3
1952–53					
67.3		I Love Lucy	CBS	M 9:00	leap in #s
54.7		Arthur Godfrey	CBS	M 8:30	
47.1		Arthur Godfrey	CBS	W 8:00	
1953–54					
58.8		I Love Lucy	CBS	M 9:00	
53.2		Dragnet	NBC	Th 9:00	
43.6		Arthur Godfrey	CBS	M 8:30	
1954–55					
49.3		I Love Lucy	CBS	M 9:00	
42.4		Jackie Gleason	CBS	Sa 8:00	
42.1		Dragnet	NBC	Th 9:00	
1955–56					
47.5		$64,000 Question	CBS	T 10:00	first year hits top 3
46.1		I Love Lucy	CBS	M 9:00	
39.5		Ed Sullivan	CBS	Su 8:00	
1956–57					
43.7		I Love Lucy	CBS	Su 6:30	
38.4		Ed Sullivan	CBS	Su 8:00	
36.9		General Electric	CBS	Su 9:00	
1957–58					
43.1		Gunsmoke	CBS	Sa 10:00	leap in #s
35.3		Danny Thomas	ABC	Th 9:00	
35.2		Tales of Wells Fargo	NBC	M 8:30	first year hits top 3
1958–59					
39.6		Gunsmoke	CBS	Sa 10:00	
36.1		Wagon Train	NBC	W 7:30	
34.3		Have Gun, Will Travel	CBS	Sa 9:30	

Chart 1 *(continued)*

Date/ Rating	Difference	Program	Network	Time Slot	Notes
1959–60					
40.3		Gunsmoke	CBS	Sa 10:00	
38.4		Wagon Train	NBC	W 7:30	
34.7		Have Gun, Will Travel	CBS	Sa 9:30	
1960–61					
37.3	3.1	Gunsmoke	CBS	Sa 10:00	first year hits top 3
34.2	3.3	Wagon Train	NBC	W 7:30	
30.9		Have Gun, Will Travel	CBS	Sa 9:30	
1961–62					
32.1	2.1	Wagon Train	NBC	W 7:30	
30.0	1.7	Bonanza	NBC	Su 9:00	
28.3		Gunsmoke	CBS	Sa 10:00	
1962–63					
36.0	4.9	Beverly Hillbillies	CBS	W 9:00	
31.1	0.0	Candid Camera	CBS	Su 10:00	
31.1		Red Skelton	CBS	T 8:30	
1963–64					
39.1	2.2	Beverly Hillbillies	CBS	W 9:00	leap in #s
36.9	3.6	Bonanza	NBC	Su 9:00	
33.3		Dick Van Dyke	CBS	W 9:30	
1964–65					
36.3	5.3	Bonanza	NBC	Su 9:00	
31.0	0.3	Bewitched	ABC	Th 9:00	first year hits top 3
30.7		Gomer Pyle	CBS	F 9:30	first year hits top 3
1965–66					
31.8	4.0	Bonanza	NBC	Su 9:00	
27.8	0.1	Gomer Pyle	CBS	F 9:00	
27.7		Lucy Show	CBS	M 8:30	
1966–67					
29.1	0.9	Bonanza	NBC	Su 9:00	
28.2	0.8	Red Skelton	CBS	T 8:30	
27.4		Andy Griffith	CBS	M 9:00	
1967–68					
27.6	0.6	Andy Griffith	CBS	M 9:00	
27.0	1.4	Lucy Show	CBS	M 8:30	
25.6		Gomer Pyle	CBS	F 8:30	

(continued)

Chart 1 *(continued)*

Date/ Rating	Difference	Program	Network	Time Slot	Notes
1968–69					
31.8	4.6	Rowan & Martin	NBC	M 8:00	first year hits top 3
27.2	0.6	Gomer Pyle	CBS	F 8:30	
26.6		Bonanza	NBC	Su 9:00	
1969–70					
26.3	0.4	Rowan & Martin	NBC	M 8:00	
25.9	1.1	Gunsmoke	CBS	M 7:30	
24.8		Bonanza	NBC	Su 9:00	
1970–71					
29.6	1.7	Marcus Welby	ABC	T 10:00	
27.9	1.8	Flip Wilson	NBC	Th 7:30	first year hits top 3
26.1		Here's Lucy	CBS	M 8:30	
1971–72					
34.0	5.8	All in the Family	CBS	T 9:30/ Sa 8:00	first year hits top 3
28.2	0.4	Flip Wilson	NBC	Th 7:30	
27.8		Marcus Welby	ABC	T 10:00	
1972–73					
33.3	5.7	All in the Family	CBS	Su 8:00	
27.6	2.4	Sanford & Son	NBC	F 8:00	first year hits top 3
25.2		Hawaii 5-O	CBS	T 8:30	
1973–74					
31.2	3.2	All in the Family	CBS	Sa 8:00	
28.0	0.5	Waltons	CBS	Th 8:00	
27.5		Sanford & Son	NBC	F 8:00	
1974–75					
30.2	0.6	All in the Family	CBS	Sa 8:00	
29.6	1.1	Sanford & Son	NBC	F 8:00	
28.5		Chico and the Man	NBC	F 8:30	first year hits top 3
1975–76					
30.1	2.1	All in the Family	CBS	M 9:00	
28.0	0.8	Rich Man, Poor Man	ABC	M 10:00	first year hits top 3
27.5		Laverne & Shirley	ABC	T 8:30	first year hits top 3
1976–77					
31.5	0.6	Happy Days	ABC	T 8:00	leap in #s
30.9	4.9	Laverne & Shirley	ABC	T 8:30	leap in #s
26.0		ABC Monday Movie	ABC	M	

Chart 1 *(continued)*

Date/ Rating	Difference	Program	Network	Time Slot	Notes
1977–78					
31.6	0.2	Laverne & Shirley	ABC	T 8:30	
31.4	3.1	Happy Days	ABC	T 8:00	
28.3		Three's Company	ABC	Th 9:30/ T 9:00	first year hits top 3
1978–79					
30.5	0.2	Laverne & Shirley	ABC	T 8:30	
30.3	1.7	Three's Company	ABC	T 9:00	
28.6		Mork & Mindy	ABC	Th 8:00	first year hits top 3
1979–80					
28.4	2.2	60 Minutes	CBS	Su 7:00	
26.2	0.4	Three's Company	ABC	T 9:00	
25.8		That's Incredible	ABC	M 8:00	first year hits top 3
1980–81					
34.5	7.2	Dallas	CBS	F 10:00	leap in #s
27.3	0.3	Dukes of Hazzard	CBS	F 9:00	
27.0		60 Minutes	CBS	Su 7:00	
1981–82					
28.4	0.7	Dallas	CBS	F 9:00	
27.7	4.3	60 Minutes	CBS	Su 7:00	
23.4		Jeffersons	CBS	Su 9:30	
1982–83					
25.5	0.9	60 Minutes	CBS	Su 7:00	
24.6	2.0	Dallas	CBS	F 9:00	
22.6		M*A*S*H	CBS	M 9:00	
1983–84					
25.7	1.5	Dallas	CBS	F 9:00	
24.2	0.1	60 Minutes	CBS	Su 7:00	
24.1		Dynasty	ABC	W 9:00	
1984–85					
25.0	0.3	Dynasty	ABC	W 9:00	
24.7	0.5	Dallas	CBS	F 9:00	
24.2		The Cosby Show	NBC	Th 8:00	
1985–86					
33.7	3.7	The Cosby Show	NBC	Th 8:00	leap in #s
30.0	4.7	Family Ties	NBC	Th 8:30	leap in #s
25.3		Murder, She Wrote	CBS	Su 8:00	

(continued)

Chart 1 *(continued)*

Date/Rating	Difference	Program	Network	Time Slot	Notes
1986–87					
34.9	2.2	The Cosby Show	NBC	Th 8:00	
32.7	5.5	Family Ties	NBC	Th 8:30	
27.2		Cheers	NBC	Th 9:00	
1987–88					
27.8	2.8	The Cosby Show	NBC	Th 8:00	
25.0	1.6	Different World	NBC	Th 8:30	first year hits top 3
23.4		Cheers	NBC	Th 9:00	
1988–89					
25.8	4.6	The Cosby Show	NBC	Th 8:00	
23.6	0.7	Roseanne	ABC	T 8:30/ T 9:00	first year hits top 3
22.9		Different World	NBC	Th 8:30	
1989–90					
23.1	0.0	The Cosby Show	NBC	Th 8:00	
23.1	0.1	Roseanne	ABC	T 9:00	
23.0		Different World	NBC	Th 8:30	
1990–91					
21.3	0.7	Cheers	NBC	Th 9:00	
20.6	2.5	60 Minutes	CBS	Su 7:00	
18.1		Roseanne	ABC	T 9:00	
1991–92					
21.9	1.0	60 Minutes	CBS	Su 7:00	
19.9	1.3	Roseanne	ABC	T 9:00	
18.6		Murphy Brown	CBS	M 9:00	
1992–93					
21.9	1.2	60 Minutes	CBS	Su 7:00	
20.7	1.3	Roseanne	ABC	T 9:00	
19.4		Home Improvement	ABC	W 9:00	
1993–94					
20.9	0.9	60 Minutes	CBS	Su 7:00	
20.4	1.0	Home Improvement	ABC	W 9:00/ W 8:00	
19.4		Seinfeld	NBC	Th 9:00	
1994–95					
20.6	0.6	Seinfeld	NBC	Th 9:00	
20.0	0.5	ER	NBC	Th 10:00	first year hits top 3
19.5		Home Improvement	ABC	T 9:00	

Chart 1 *(continued)*

Date/ Rating	Difference	Program	Network	Time Slot	Notes
1995–96					
22.0	0.8	ER	NBC	Th 10:00	
21.2	2.5	Seinfeld	NBC	Th 9:00	
18.7		Friends	NBC	Th 8:00	
1996–97					
		ER	NBC	Th 10:00	
		Seinfeld	NBC	Th 9:00	
		Friends	NBC	Th 8:00	
1997–98					
		Seinfeld	NBC	Th 9:00	
		ER	NBC	Th 10:00	
		Veronica's Closet	NBC	Th 9:30	

imply that people weren't just watching whatever was on (the LOP tendency), but that they had gone somewhat out of their way to tune in. These programs with out-of-the-normal ratings I refer to as ratings busters or blockbusters, and they include both sitcoms and other genres. They are *The Beverly Hillbillies, Bonanza, Rowan & Martin's Laugh-In, All in the Family, Laverne & Shirley* (with *Happy Days*), *Dallas,* and *The Cosby Show*. Because these programs may not be the ones many people would have predicted to fit the category of being a blockbuster (why isn't my favorite program here?), and because a review of these will also eliminate various speculations as to the cause of the blockbuster phenomenon, I wish to discuss the data in more specific detail.

The first program of the 1960s to secure an unusually large rating relative to its peers was *The Beverly Hillbillies*, in the 1962–63 season. For the year, *The Beverly Hillbillies* rated 36.0. Moreover, that rating was 4.9 points over its rivals,

Candid Camera and *The Red Skelton Show*. *The Beverly Hillbillies* did well the following year (39.1 to *Bonanza*'s 36.9 and *The Dick Van Dyke Show*'s 33.3); however, the differential between these programs does drop to 2.2 and 5.8, respectively.

During the mid-1960s, *Bonanza*, like *The Beverly Hillbillies*, did very well. In 1964–65, it was 5.3 points over second-place *Bewitched* and 5.6 points more than third-place *Gomer Pyle, U.S.M.C.* The following year, *Bonanza*'s ratings were 31.8, 4.0 points over *Gomer Pyle, U.S.M.C.*, and 4.1 over *The Lucy Show*. Within the notion of "must-see TV," *Bonanza* (and also *Dallas*), like the four situation comedies that I will study, counts as a ratings buster. In 1968–69, *Rowan & Martin's Laugh-In* managed to rate 4.6 points over the second-place *Gomer Pyle, U.S.M.C.*, and 5.2 over third-place *Bonanza*. While *Gomer Pyle, U.S.M.C.*, and *Bonanza* remained popular, their strengths waned, and *Rowan & Martin's Laugh-In* dropped the following year to a more normal 26.3, 0.4 points over second-place *Gunsmoke*.

The next major "blip" on the ratings chart arrived with *All in the Family* during the 1971–72 season. *All in the Family* pushed ratings for the top-rated programs back up into the 30s (they had fallen predominantly into the upper 20s in the mid-1960s, with only two programs securing a low 30 for a season average). *All in the Family* not only commanded a 34.0 in 1971–72, but held steady at 33.3 in 1972–73, 31.2 in 1973–74, 30.2 in 1974–75, and 30.1 in 1975–76. The first programs after *All in the Family*'s 1971–72 record to reach the 30s were *Happy Days'* 31.5 and *Laverne & Shirley*'s 30.9 in 1976–77. Truly the early 1970s belonged to *All in the Fam-*

ily. In 1971–72, *All in the Family* not only broke the ratings back into the 30s, but the program rated 5.8 points over second-place *The Flip Wilson Show* and 6.2 points over *Marcus Welby, M.D.* Moreover, it held a commanding-to-strong lead for five seasons.

Happy Days and, more appropriately as I shall argue in chapter 4, its spin-off *Laverne & Shirley* were the next major blockbusters. In 1976–77, the duo rated 5.5 points over third-ranked *ABC Monday Night Movie.* The following season saw a decline for the programs, but they still rated in the low 30s versus a 28.3 for *Three's Company*, and *Laverne & Shirley* held onto first place and a 30.5 through 1978–79 while leading the ABC pack of *Three's Company* (30.3), spin-off *Mork & Mindy* (28.6), and *Happy Days* (28.6).

The "Who Shot J.R.?" plotline pushed *Dallas* into a ratings peak in 1980–81. At 34.5 over second-place *The Dukes of Hazzard, Dallas* outranked its rivals by 7.2 points and more. However, *Dallas* dropped quickly the following year to 28.4, only 0.7 points over second-place *60 Minutes.*

During the early 1980s, the top-rated programs held in the mid-20 figures. But in 1985–86, *The Cosby Show* once again produced a peak, pulling with it second-ranked *Family Ties* which followed *The Cosby Show* in the NBC Thursday night lineup. *The Cosby Show*'s 33.7 rating once more dragged the top numbers back into the low 30s, and *Family Ties* contributed a 30.0 to exceed third-rated *Murder, She Wrote* by 4.7 points. *The Cosby Show* and *Family Ties* held their position in 1986–87, with ratings of 34.9 and 32.7 over third-place *Cheers* at 27.2. By 1987–88, however, *The Cosby Show* had dropped down to the upper 20s, and the following

season, 1988–89, dropped to 25.8, although beating out second-place *Roseanne* by 4.6 points. *Roseanne* went on the following year to tie with *The Cosby Show* for first place. Here
the profound effects of cable broadcasting and the VCR revolution were altering the dynamics of television viewing, however, and from the early 1990s, top-rated network programs
manage to secure a rating of about 20, with other shows in the
teens. Not only are the ratings at their lowest level, however,
but ratings are less meaningful. From this point on (ca. 1990),
using ratings to determine unusual cultural currency is no
longer possible because of time-shifting and the practice of
running programs still in production in syndication on channels other than the four to five major networks. I shall return
to this post-1990 situation in the epilogue, and expand on its
implications for television viewing.

Lest you hypothesize erroneous explanations for the blockbuster phenomenon, let me eliminate some possibilities. Can
the blockbuster be explained by time or night of first airing? At the height of their popularity, *I Love Lucy* ran at
9 P.M. Mondays; *Bonanza* 9 P.M. Sundays; *Beverly Hillbillies*
9 P.M. Wednesdays; *All in the Family* 9:30 P.M. Tuesdays, then
8 P.M. Saturdays; *Happy Days/Laverne & Shirley* 8 P.M. Tuesdays; *Dallas* 10 P.M. Fridays; and *The Cosby Show* 8 P.M.
Thursdays.

Perhaps the runaway hit had little competition. *I Love
Lucy* ran opposite the *ABC All Star News*, *Guide Right*, and
Hollywood Opening Night. *Beverly Hillbillies* had strong
competitors in *Going My Way* and *Perry Como's Kraft Music
Hall*. *All in the Family* ran against *Getting Together* and *The
Partners*. *Happy Days* went up against *Tony Orlando and*

Dawn and *Baa Baa Black Sheep*. While none of these alternative shows are really tough, they are moderately normal competition for television.

Perhaps the popularity has something to do with immediate resonance or topicality with the TV-viewing audience. That answer doesn't work either since the programs took a variable amount of time to reach number one status. *The Beverly Hillbillies* took only about four weeks to reach number one, beating out *The Lucille Ball Show*. *All in the Family* remained low in the ratings after its January 1971 first half-season. It started the first week of the fall 1971–72 season in twelfth place and then the following week went to number one, floating in the top figures thereafter. *Laverne & Shirley*, buoyed by the lead-in *Happy Days* which had a slow build over two years, hit number one its premiere episode in January 1976. It shared first-place honors off and on all of the rest of the season with *Happy Days*. Finally, *The Cosby Show* started in the top ten in the fall of 1984 and was first by January 1985. It ended third overall that season and then held seasonal first place for five more years.[15] It is the case, though, that all of the ratings-busting series do hit blockbuster status within one year of their premiere.

As I indicated, my project is to examine the phenomenon of programs that secure sufficient ratings to suggest a "must-see" behavior within the U.S. population. *Bonanza* in the mid-1960s, *Rowan & Martin's Laugh-In* in 1968–69, and *Dallas* in 1980–81 would count as such given their excessive numbers relative to their competitors. I have chosen to focus on the four half-hour comedies, however, because they obviously were producing a going-out-of-one's-way activity. *Bonanza* was an institution, perpetuated in part by its time slot on NBC Sunday evenings at 9 P.M. and in part by the general popularity of the family melodramatic western in the late 1950s and early 1960s. *Dallas*, another hour-long melodrama, provoked its high numbers as a result of a gimmick, and while remaining popular and even ranking number one for one season, dropped quickly off to numbers in the high 20s, more comparable with those of its competitors. *Rowan & Martin's Laugh-In*, also an hour-long program, likewise was a one-season ratings buster. However, it is the case that all three of those programs meet my general criteria for blockbusters.

Another set of statistics, although not particularly justifying the limits of my study, provides information about the influence of these selected programs on the general programming and viewing of television. Chart 2 lists all of the top ten programs year by year, with the situation comedies in bold italic. One reason to examine a ratings-busting program is to see any spillover effect of its popularity, whether it spawned imitations or general viewer refocusing on the genre. In each sitcom case, the successful program turned around the numbers for the genre. That is, the ratings buster altered the generic composition of the top ten programs to increase significantly the overall number of sitcoms. Although *Dallas*, of course, did this too, with *Dynasty* and *Falcon Crest* becoming highly successful in the early 1980s TV lineup, neither *Bonanza* nor *Rowan & Martin's Laugh-In* stimulated competitive programs that broke into the top ten.

However, *The Beverly Hillbillies* yielded *Petticoat Junction* (fourth in 1963–64) and headed a high tide of half-hour comedy programs: in 1962–63, five of the top ten were situation comedies; in 1963–64 seven were; in 1964–65 five; and in 1965–66 eight.

Likewise, *All in the Family* resulted in *Sanford and Son, Maude, Chico and the Man, The Jeffersons,* and some would argue the "new relevance" sitcoms of *The Mary Tyler Moore Show, Bridget Loves Bernie, M*A*S*H, Rhoda,* and *Good Times* (just listing ones in the top ten for the next few years). Moreover, *All in the Family* preceded a vigorous return of the sitcom by arriving in a season in which only one of the top ten programs was a half-hour comedy (1970–71). Not only did *All in the Family* dramatically alter the top ten landscape, but it started a decade in which sitcoms accounted for over half of the top ten programs through the 1970–80 seasons: 55 out of 101 programs.

Laverne & Shirley, as a spin-off of *Happy Days,* was unique in pulling its parent into the preeminent position they both held for four seasons. Spin-offs and imitators of these programs included *Three's Company, Mork & Mindy,* and *The Ropers. Laverne & Shirley* and *Happy Days* participated in the 1970s sitcom dominance, of course, with the second half of the decade run by the kidvid version of the genre.

Finally, *The Cosby Show* purposefully used its strength to start *A Different World,* which secured second place in its first season, riding on its father's coattails. Earlier, *The Cosby Show* produced a surge for *Family Ties* and *Cheers,* and also generated obvious imitators such as *Growing Pains* and *The Wonder Years. The Cosby Show* has been widely described as the program that resurrected what

CHART 2
Top Ten Programs, 1960–

	1960–61	1961–62	1962–63	1963–64	1964–65
1	Gunsmoke	Wagon Train	*Beverly Hillbillies*	*Beverly Hillbillies*	Bonanza
2	Wagon Train	Bonanza	2tCandid Camera	Bonanza	*Bewitched*
3	Have Gun, Will Travel	Gunsmoke	2tRed Skelton Show	*Dick Van Dyke Show*	*Gomer Pyle, U.S.M.C.*
4	*Andy Griffith Show*	*Hazel*	4tBonanza	Petticoat Junction	*Andy Griffith Show*
5	*The Real McCoys*	Perry Mason	*4tLucy Show*	*Andy Griffith Show*	The Fugitive
6	Rawhide	Red Skelton Show	*Andy Griffith Show*	*Lucy Show*	Red Skelton Hour
7	Candid Camera	*Andy Griffith Show*	7tBen Casey	Candid Camera	*Dick Van Dyke Show*
8	8Untouchables	*Danny Thomas Show*	*7tDanny Thomas Show*	Ed Sullivan Show	*Lucy Show*
9	8Price is Right	Dr. Kildare	*Dick Van Dyke Show*	*Danny Thomas Show*	Peyton Place II
10	*Jack Benny Show*	Candid Camera	Gunsmoke	*My Favorite Martian*	Combat

	1965–66	1966–67	1967–68	1968–69	1969–70
1	Bonanza	Bonanza	*Andy Griffith Show*	Rowan & Martin's	Rowan & Martin's
2	*Gomer Pyle, U.S.M.C.*	Red Skelton Hour	*Lucy Show*	*Gomer Pyle, U.S.M.C.*	Gunsmoke
3	*Lucy Show*	*Andy Griffith Show*	*Gomer Pyle, U.S.M.C.*	Bonanza	Bonanza
4	Red Skelton Hour	*Lucy Show*	4tGunsmoke	*Mayberry R.F.D.*	*Mayberry R.F.D.*
5	*Batman (Thurs)*	*Jackie Gleason Show*	*4tFamily Affair*	*Family Affair*	*Family Affair*
6	*Andy Griffith Show*	Green Acres	4tBonanza	Gunsmoke	*Here's Lucy*
7	*7tBewitched*	7tDaktari	Red Skelton Show	*Julia*	Red Skelton Hour
8	*7tBeverly Hillbillies*	*7tBewitched*	Dean Martin Show	Dean Martin Show	Marcus Welby, M.D.
9	Hogan's Heroes	*Beverly Hillbillies*	*Jackie Gleason Show*	Here's Lucy	Walt Disney's Wond
10	*Batman (Wed)*	*Gomer Pyle, U.S.M.C.*	Sat Night at Movies	*Beverly Hillbillies*	*Doris Day Show*

	1970–71	1971–72	1972–73	1973–74	1974–75
1	Marcus Welby, M.D.	All in the Family	All in the Family	All in the Family	All in the Family
2	Flip Wilson Show	Flip Wilson Show	Sanford and Son	Waltons	Sanford and Son
3	Here's Lucy	Marcus Welby, M.D.	Hawaii Five-O	Sanford and Son	Chico and the Man
4	Ironside	Gunsmoke	Maude	M*A*S*H	The Jeffersons
5	Gunsmoke	ABC Movie of Week	5tBridget Loves Bernie	Hawaii Five-O	M*A*S*H
6	ABC Movie of Week	Sanford and Son	5tNBC Sun Mystery	Maude	Rhoda
7	Hawaii Five-O	Mannix	7tMary Tyler Moore	7tKojak	Good Times
8	Medical Center	8tFunny Face	7tGunsmoke	7tSonny and Cher	Waltons
9	Bonanza	8tAdam 12	Wonderful World	9tMary Tyler Moore	Maude
10	The F.B.I.	10tMary Tyler Moore	Ironside	9tCannon	Hawaii Five-O
		10tHere's Lucy			

	1975–76	1976–77	1977–78	1978–79	1979–80
1	All in the Family	Happy Days	Laverne & Shirley	Laverne & Shirley	60 Minutes
2	Rich Man, Poor Man	Laverne & Shirley	Happy Days	Three's Company	Three's Company
3	Laverne & Shirley	ABC Mon Night Movie	Three's Company	3tMork & Mindy	That's Incredible
4	Maude	M*A*S*H	4t60 Minutes	3tHappy Days	4tAlice
5	Bionic Woman	Charlie's Angels	4tCharlie's Angels	Angie	4tM*A*S*H
6	Phyllis	Big Event	4tAll in the Family	60 Minutes	Dallas
7	7tSanford and Son	Six Million Dollar Man	Little House on Prairie	M*A*S*H	Flo
8	7tRhoda	8tABC Sun Night Movie	8tAlice	The Ropers	The Jeffersons
9	Six Million Dollar Man	8tBaretta	8tM*A*S*H	9tAll in the Family	Dukes of Hazzard
10	ABC Mon Night Movie	8tOne Day at a Time	One Day at a Time	9tTaxi	One Day at a Time

(continued)

Chart 2 (continued)

	1980–81	1981–82	1982–83	1983–84	1984–85
1	Dallas	Dallas	60 Minutes	Dallas	Dynasty
2	Dukes of Hazzard	60 Minutes	Dallas	60 Minutes	Dallas
3	60 Minutes	The Jeffersons	3tM*A*S*H	Dynasty	Cosby Show
4	M*A*S*H	Three's Company	3tMagnum, P.I.	A-Team	60 Minutes
5	Love Boat	Alice	Dynasty	Simon & Simon	Family Ties
6	The Jeffersons	6tDukes of Hazzard	Three's Company	Magnum, P.I.	A-Team
7	Alice	6tToo Close for Comfort	Simon & Simon	Falcon Crest	Simon & Simon
8	8tHouse Calls	ABC Mon Night Movie	Falcon Crest	Kate & Allie	Murder, She Wrote
9	8tThree's Company	M*A*S*H	Love Boat	Hotel	Knots Landing
10	Little House on Prairie	One Day at a Time	A-Team	Cagney & Lacey	Falcon Crest

	1985–86	1986–87	1987–88	1988–89	1989–90
1	Cosby Show	Cosby Show	Cosby Show	Cosby Show	1tCosby Show
2	Family Ties	Family Ties	A Different World	Roseanne	1tRoseanne
3	Murder, She Wrote	Cheers	Cheers	Different World	Cheers
4	60 Minutes	Murder, She Wrote	Golden Girls	Cheers	Different World
5	Cheers	Golden Girls	Growing Pains	60 Minutes	Amer's Home Videos
6	Dallas	60 Minutes	Who's the Boss?	Golden Girls	Golden Girls
7	7tDynasty	Night Court	Night Court	Who's the Boss?	60 Minutes
8	7tGolden Girls	Growing Pains	60 Minutes	Murder, She Wrote	Wonder Years
9	Miami Vice	Moonlighting	Murder, She Wrote	Empty Nest	Empty Nest
10	Who's the Boss?	Who's the Boss?	10tAlf	Anything but Love	Mon Night Football
			10tWonder Years		

#	1990–91	1991–92	1992–93	1993–94	1994–95
1	Cheers	60 Minutes	60 Minutes	60 Minutes	Seinfeld
2	60 Minutes	Roseanne	Roseanne	Home Improvement	ER
3	Roseanne	Murphy Brown	Home Improvement	Seinfeld	Home Improvement
4	Different World	4tCheers	Murphy Brown	Roseanne	Grace Under Fire
5	Cosby Show	4tHome Improvement	Murder, She Wrote	Grace Under Fire	Mon Night Football
6	Murphy Brown	Designing Women	Coach	Coach	60 Minutes
7	7tEmpty Nest	Full House	Mon Night Football	Frasier	N.Y.P.D. Blue
8	7tAmer's Home Videos	Murder, She Wrote	8tCBS Sun Movie	Mon Night Football	8tMurder, She Wrote
9	Mon Night Football	Major Dad	8tCheers	Murphy Brown	8tFriends
10	Golden Girls	10tCoach	Full Horse	CBS Sun Movie	Roseanne
		10tRoom for Two			

#	1995–96	1996–97	1997–98
1	ER	ER	Seinfeld
2	Seinfeld	Seinfeld	ER
3	Friends	Friends	Veronica's Closet
4	Caroline in the City	Suddenly Susan	Friends
5	Mon Night Football	The Naked Truth	Touched by an Angel
6	The Single Guy	Fired Up	Mon Night Football
7	Home Improvement	Mon Night Football	Union Square
8	Boston Common	Home Improvement	60 Minutes
9	60 Minutes	The Single Guy	CBS Surday Movie
10	NYPD Blue	Touched by an Angel	Home Improvement

appeared to be a dying genre (although this is a highly suspect declaration). It is the case that the year preceding *The Cosby Show*'s arrival, *Kate & Allie* was the only sitcom in the top ten programs. *The Cosby Show* and *Family Ties* entered these ranks in 1984–85, and then another wave of sitcom dominance held for the following decade. Between the 1984–85 season and the 1994–95 season, 70 of the 102 top ten programs were situation comedies. This decade did witness, like the decade of 1971–80, some varying subtypes of the genre, with programs such as *The Wonder Years* and some episodes of *Roseanne* and *Murphy Brown* breaching boundaries between comedy and drama. Chart 3, which traces the start and end dates and the ratings for all top ten sitcoms, provides a final indication of the strength and longevity of the sitcom on prime-time television. It also helps to see the influences that the ratings-buster sitcom has on the subtypes of the genre.

Thus, while this book might be devoted to all seven ratings busters, the overall impact of the four situation comedies on the schedule and flow of television helps justify restricting the study to them. Moreover, comparing the consequences of success for programs within generally the same genre makes a neater study. As David Marc points out:

The situation comedy has proven to be the most durable of all commercial television genres. Other types of programming that have appeared to be staples of prime-time fare at various junctures in TV history have seen their heyday and faded (the western, the comedy-variety show, and the big-money quiz show among them). The sitcom, however, has remained a consistent and ubiquitous feature of prime-time network schedules since the premiere of *Mary Kay and Johnny* on DuMont in 1947.[16]

As Marc's remark indicates, the success of the half-hour comedy within U.S. prime-time broadcasting has not gone unnoticed. Numerous observations to account for this have been offered, and four types of explanations contribute to an overall explanation. As I will suggest, however, none of these traditional hypotheses explains the blockbuster phenomenon. For that, I will turn to other theory.[17]

One of the most obvious possible explanations for the success of the situation comedy is that the genre fits the medium. This is a classic "media specificity" claim in which the thesis is that a medium has a particular ontological nature and that that ontology coincides with a particular content. Such a media specificity hypothesis in film theory implies that certain techniques of cinema are particularly cinematic—the long take (André Bazin) or the close-up (the French writers of the 1920s). Or that crowds and masses of people or objects in motion (Siegfried Kracauer) fit the medium's inherent nature.

To lodge media specificity claims for television repeats the process common to most new technologies in which their supporters try to mark them out as novel and revolutionary.[18] Not all theories about the specificity of broadcast television work for the prime-time sitcom, however—but some do, and these have been proposed to explain its success. For example, Barry Curtis proposes that television is about entertainment as opposed to "work, education, seriousness."[19] Thus, "television in most of its manifestations asserts the importance of humor and the humorousness of everyday life—even the tail end of the news broadcasts seems to be shaped to the good humored flow of television continuity" (p. 11). Curtis writes in an anthology devoted to British television where the public-service imperative is much stronger than for U.S. commercial

CHART 3
Longevity and Ratings of Top 25 Sitcoms, 1949–

Group 1, 1949–1966

Program	Start	1949–50	1950–51	1951–52	1952–53	1953–54	1954–55	1955–56	1956–57	1957–58	1958–59	1959–60	1960–61	1961–62	1962–63	1963–64	1964–65	1965–66	End
Mama — CBS (rank)	Jul-49		10	11	18														Jul-56
Mama — CBS (rating)			39.7	41.3	37.0														
Life of Riley — NBC (rank)	Oct-49			16		13	21	21											Aug-58
Life of Riley — NBC (rating)				37.4		35.0	30.9	30.1											
George Burns/Allen — CBS (rank)	Oct-50					20													Sep-58
George Burns/Allen — CBS (rating)						32.4													
Jack Benny — CBS (rank)	Oct-50			9	12	16	7	5	10				10		11	12			Sep-65
Jack Benny — CBS (rating)				42.8	39.0	33.3	38.3	37.2	32.3				26.2		26.2	25.0			
Amos 'n' Andy — CBS (rank)	Jun-51			13	25														Jun-53
Amos 'n' Andy — CBS (rating)				38.9	34.4														
I Love Lucy — CBS (rank)	Oct-51			3	1	1	1	2	1										Sep-61
I Love Lucy — CBS (rating)				50.9	67.3	58.8	49.3	46.1	43.7										
Life with Luigi — CBS (rank)	Sep-52				13														Jun-53
Life with Luigi — CBS (rating)					38.5														
Our Miss Brooks — CBS (rank)	Oct-52				22	14													Sep-56
Our Miss Brooks — CBS (rating)					35.0	34.2													
I Married Joan — NBC (rank)	Oct-52				25														Apr-55
I Married Joan — NBC (rating)					30.2														

	Start	1949–50	1950–51	1951–52	1952–53	1953–54	1954–55	1955–6	1956–57	1957–58	1958–59	1959–60	1960–61	1961–62	1962–63	1963–64	1964–65	1965–66	End
Private Sec/Ann Sou	Feb-53					24	19	12	25			21	24						Oct-57
CBS						30.3	32.2	34.–	29.0			27.0	24.2						Sep-61
Danny Thomas	Sep-53								2	5	4	12			8	7	9		Sep-65
CBS									35.3	32.8	31.1	25.9			26.1	28.7	26.7		
Father Knows Best	Oct-54									23	13	6							Apr-63
CBS/NBC/CBS/A										27.7	28.3	29.7							
December Bride	Oct-54						10	6	5	9									Apr-61
CBS							34.7	37.0	35.2	30.7									
Phil Silvers	Sep-55								22										Sep-59
CBS									29.7										
Honeymooners	Oct-55							19											Sep-56
CBS								30.2											
Gale Storm Show	Sep-56									16									Mar-60
CBS										28.8									
Real McCoys	Oct-57										8	11	5		14				Sep-63
ABC											30.1	28.2	27.7		24.2				
Donna Reed	Sep-58															16			Sep-66
ABC																24.5			
Many Loves/D Gillis	Sep-59												23	21					Sep-63
CBS												23.0	22.9						
Dennis the Menace	Oct-59											16							Sep-63
CBS												26.0							

NOTE: "Ozzie and Harriet" and "Leave It to Beaver" never ranked in top 25

(continued)

Group 2, 1960–1974

	Start	1960-61	1961-62	1962-63	1963-64	1964-65	1965-66	1966-67	1967-68	1968-69	1969-70	1970-71	1971-72	1972-73	1973-74	End
My Three Sons	Sep-60	13	11			13	15		24	14	15	19				Aug-72
ABC		25.8	24.7			25.5	23.8		20.8	22.8	21.8	20.8				
Flintstones	Sep-60	18	21													Sep-66
ABC		24.3	22.9													
Andy Griffith/Mayb	Oct-60	4	7	6	5	4	6	3	1	4	4					Sep-71
CBS		27.8	27.0	29.7	29.4	28.3	26.9	27.4	27.6	25.4	24.4					
Hazel	Sep-61		4	15	22											Sep-66
NBC			27.7	25.1	22.8											
Car 54, Where are?	Sep-61		20													Sep-63
NBC			23.2													
Dick Van Dyke	Oct-61			9	3	7	16									Sep-66
CBS				27.1	33.3	27.1	23.6									
Beverly Hillbillies	Sep-62			1	1	12	7	9	12	10	18					Sep-71
CBS				36.0	39.1	25.6	25.9	23.4	23.3	23.5	21.7					
Lucy Show/Here's L	Oct-62			4	6	8	3	4	2	9	6	3	10	15		Sep-74
CBS				29.8	28.1	26.6	27.7	26.2	27.0	23.8	23.9	26.1	23.7	21.9		
McHale's Navy	Oct-62				22											Aug-66
ABC					22.8											
Petticoat Junction	Sep-63				4	15	21	23								Sep-70
CBS					30.3	25.2	22.3	20.9								
My Favorite Martian	Sep-63				10	24										Sep-66
CBS					26.3	23.7										
Patty Duke	Sep-63				18											Aug-66
ABC					23.9											
Addams Family	Sep-64					23										Sep-66
ABC						23.9										

	Start	1960–61	1961–62	1962–63	1963–64	1964–65	1965–66	1966–67	1967–68	1968–69	1969–70	1970–71	1971–72	1972–73	1973–74	End
Bewitched ABC	Sep-64					2 31.0	7 25.9	7 23.4	11 23.5	11 23.3	24 20.6					Sep-72
Gomer Pyle, USMC CBS	Sep-64					3 30.7	2 27.8	10 22.8	3 25.6	2 27.2						Sep-70
Gilligan's Island CBS	Sep-64					18 24.7	22 22.1									Sep-67
Munsters CBS	Sep-64					18 24.7										Sep-66
Hogan's Heroes CBS	Sep-65						9 24.9	17 21.8								Jul-71
Green Acres CBS	Sep-65						11 24.6	6 24.6	15 22.8	19 21.6						Sep-71
Get Smart NBC	Sep-65						12 24.5	22 21.0								Sep-70
Batman (Thurs) ABC	Jan-66						5 27.0									Mar-68
Batman (Wed) ABC	Jan-66						10 24.7									Mar-68
Family Affair CBS	Sep-66							14 22.6	4 25.5	5 25.2	5 24.2					Sep-71
Julia NBC	Sep-68									7 24.6						May-71
Doris Day CBS	Sep-68									10 22.8	20 22.7	23 21.2				Sep-73
Bill Cosby NBC	Sep-69									11 22.7						Aug-71

(continued)

Group 3, 1970–1985

	Start	1970-71	1971-72	1972-73	1973-74	1974-75	1975-76	1976-77	1977-78	1978-79	1979-80	1980-81	1981-82	1982-83	1983-84	1984-85	End
Mary Tyler Moore	Sep-70	22	10	7	9	11	19										Sep-77
CBS		20.3	23.7	26.6	23.1	24.0	21.9										
Partridge Family	Sep-70	25	16	19													Aug-74
ABC		19.8	22.6	20.6													
All in the Family/A's	Jan-71		1	1	1	1	1	12	4	9	11	13	12	22			Sep-83
CBS			34.0	33.3	31.2	30.2	30.1	22.9	24.4	24.9	22.9	21.4	21.6	18.3			
Funny Face	Sep-71		8.0														Dec-71
CBS			23.9														
New Dick Van Dyke	Sep-71		18.0														Sep-74
CBS			22.2														
Sanford & Son	Jan-72		6	2	3	2	7										Sep-77
NBC			25.2	27.6	27.5	29.6	24.4										
M*A*S*H	Sep-72				4	5	14	4	8	7	4	4	9	3			Sep-83
CBS					25.7	27.4	22.9	25.9	23.2	25.4	25.3	25.7	22.3	22.6			
Maude	Sep-72			4	6	9	4										Apr-78
CBS				24.7	23.5	24.9	25.0										
Bridget Loves Bernie	Sep-72			5													Sep-73
CBS				24.2													
Bob Newhart	Sep-72			16	12	17											Aug-78
CBS				21.8	22.3	22.4											
Brian Keith	Sep-72			25													Aug-74
NBC				19.9													
Good Times	Jan-74				17	7	24										Aug-79
ABC					21.4	25.8	21.0										
Chico and the Man	Sep-74					3	25										Jul-78
NBC						28.5	20.8										

	Start	1970-71	1971-72	1972-73	1973-74	1974-75	1975-76	1976-77	1977-78	1978-79	1979-80	1980-81	1981-82	1982-83	1983-84	1984-85	End
Rhoda	Sep-74					6	7	25									Dec-78
CBS						26.3	24.4	20.1									
Paul Sand	Sep-74					25											Jan-75
CBS						20.7											
The Jeffersons	Jan-75					4	21	42			8	6	3	12	19		Jul-85
CBS						27.6	21.5	21.0			24.3	23.5	23.4	20.0	18.6		
Barney Miller	Jan-75							17	17	15	20						Sep-82
ABC								22.2	21.4	22.6	20.9						
Phyllis	Sep-75						6										Aug-77
CBS							24.5										
Welcome Back, Kot	Sep-75						18	13									Aug-79
ABC							22.1	22.7									
One Day at a Time	Dec-75						12	8	10	18	10	11	10	16			Sep-84
CBS							23.1	23.4	23.0	21.6	23.0	22.0	22.0	19.1			

Group 4, 1973–1988

	Start	1973-74	1974-75	1975-76	1976-77	1977-78	1978-79	1979-80	1980-81	1981-82	1982-83	1983-84	1984-85	1985-86	1986-87	1987-88	End
Happy Days	Jan-74	16		11	1	2	4	17	15	18							Jul-84
ABC		21.5		23.9	31.5	31.4	28.6	21.7	20.8	20.6							
Laverne & Shirley	Jan-76			3	2	1	1		21	20							May-83
ABC				27.5	30.9	31.6	30.5										
Good Heavens	Mar-76			16													Jun-76
ABC				22.5													
Three's Company	Mar-77				11	3	2	2	8	4	6						Aug-84
ABC					23.1	28.3	30.3	26.3	22.4	23.3	21.2						

(continued)

Group 4, 1973–1988 (continued)

	Start	1973–74	1974–75	1975–76	1976–77	1977–78	1978–79	1979–80	1980–81	1981–82	1982–83	1983–84	1984–85	1985–86	1986–87	1987–88	End
What's Happening	Aug-76				25												Apr-79
ABC					20.9												
Alice	Aug-76					8	13	4	7	5		25					Jul-85
CBS						23.2	23.2	25.3	22.9	22.7		17.2					
Eight is Enough	Mar-77				23	12	11	12									Aug-81
ABC					21.1	22.5	24.8	22.8									
Soap	Sep-77					13	19	25									Apr-81
CBS						22	21.3	20.5									
Mork & Mindy	Sep-78						3										Jun-82
ABC							28.6										
Taxi	Sep-78						9	13									Jul-83
ABC							24.9	22.4									
WKRP in Cincinnati	Sep-78							22									Sep-82
CBS								20.7									
Diff'rent Strokes	Nov-78								17								Aug-86
NBC									20.7								
Angie	Feb-79						5										Oct-80
ABC							26.7										
The Ropers	Mar-79						8										May-80
ABC							25.2										
Facts of Life	Aug-79									24		24					Sep-88
NBC										19.1		17.3					
Benson	Sep-79							23									Aug-86
ABC								20.6									
House Calls	Dec-79							14	8	23							Sep-82
CBS								22.1	22.4	19.2							

	Start	1973-74	1974-75	1975-76	1976-77	1977-78	1978-79	1979-80	1980-81	1981-82	1982-83	1983-84	1984-85	1985-86	1986-87	1987-88	End
Flo	Mar-80							7									Jul-81
CBS								24.4									
Too Close for Comfort	Nov-80								15	6							Sep-83
ABC									20.8	22.6							
9 to 5	Mar-82									15							Oct-83
ABC										19.3							

Group 5, 1982–1995

	Start	1982-83	1983-84	1984-85	1985-86	1986-87	1987-88	1988-89	1989-90	1990-91	1991-92	1992-93	1993-94	1994-95	End
Cheers	Sep-82			13	5	3	3	3	4	1	4	8			Aug-93
NBC				19.7	23.7	27.2	23.4	22.3	22.7	21.3	17.5	16.1			
Family Ties	Sep-82			5	2	2	17								Sep-89
NBC				22.1	30.0	32.7	17.3								
Gloria	Sep-82	18													Sep-83
CBS		18.7													
Newhart	Oct-82	12	23	16	16	12	25								Sep-90
CBS		20.0	18.0	18.4	19.6	19.5	16.5								
AfterMASH	Sep-83		15												Dec-84
CBS			20.1												
Webster	Sep-83		25	25											Sep-87
ABC			17.2	17.0											
Night Court	Jan-84			20	11	7	7	21							Jul-92
NBC				17.6	20.9	23.2	20.8	16.9							

(continued)

Group 5, 1982–1995 (continued)

	Start	1982–83	1983–84	1984–85	1985–86	1986–87	1987–88	1988–89	1989–90	1990–91	1991–92	1992–93	1993–94	1994–95	End
Kate & Allie	Mar-84		8	17	14	19									Sep-89
CBS			21.9	18.3	20.0	18.3									
Cosby Show	Sep-84			3	1	1	1	1	1	5	18				Sep-92
NBC				24.2	33.7	34.9	27.8	25.6	23.1	17.1	15.0				
Who's the Boss	Sep-84				10	10	6	7	12	19					Sep-92
ABC				21.1	22.0	21.2	20.8	17.9	15.0						
The Golden Girls	Sep-85				7	5	4	6	6	10					Sep-92
NBC					21.8	24.5	21.8	21.4	20.1						
Growing Pains	Sep-85				17	8	5	13	21						Aug-92
ABC					19.5	22.7	21.3	17.6	15.4	16.5					
227	Sep-85				20	14									Jul-90
NBC					18.8	18.9									
You Again?	Feb-86				19										Mar-87
NBC					19.2										
Hogan Family	Mar-86				24		20	22							Jul-91
NBC					18.1		16.9	16.3							
Amen	Sep-86					13	15	25							Jul-91
NBC						19.4	17.5	16.2							
Alf	Sep-86						10	15							Jun-90
NBC							18.8	17.5							
Head of the Class	Sep-86						23	20							Jun-91
ABC							16.7	17.1							
Designing Women	Sep-86								22	11	6				May-93
CBS								15.3	16.5	17.3					
My Sister Sam	Oct-86					21									Apr-88
CBS						17.4									

	Start	1982-83	1983-84	1984-85	1985-86	1986-87	1987-88	1988-89	1989-90	1990-91	1991-92	1992-93	1993-94	1994-95	End
A Different World	Sep-87						2	3	4	4	17				Jul-93
NBC							25.0	23.0	21.1	17.5	15.2				
My Two Dads	Sep-87						20								Jun-90
NBC							16.9								
Full House	Sep-87							22	14	7	10		16	25	?
ABC								15.3	15.9	17.0	15.8		14.2	12.4	
Wonder Years	Mar-88						10	22	8						Sep-93
ABC															

Group 6, 1988–

	Start	1988-89	1989-90	1990-91	1991-92	1992-93	1993-94	1994-95	End
Roseanne	Oct-88	2	1	3	2	2	4	10	?
ABC		23.8	23.1	18.1	19.9	20.7	19.1	15.5	
Empty Nest	Oct-88	9	9	7	22				Jul-95
NBC		19.2	18.9	16.7	14.3				
Dear John	Oct-88	11	17						Jul-92
NBC		18.5	17.1						
Murphy Brown	Nov-88			6	3	4	9	16	?
CBS				16.9	18.6	17.9	16.3	14.1	
Coach	Feb-89		18	18	10	6	6		?
ABC			17.0	15.3	16.7	17.5	17.4		
Anything but Love	Mar-89	10							Jun-92
ABC		19.0							
Chicken Soup	Sep-89		13						Nov-89
ABC			17.7						

(continued)

Group 6, 1988– *(continued)*

	Start	1988-89	1989-90	1990-91	1991-92	1992-93	1993-94	1994-95	End
Family Matters	Sep-89			15					?
ABC				15.8					
Major Dad	Sep-89			21	9				Sep-93
CBS				14.9	16.8				
Doogie Howser, MD	Sep-89			24					Jul-93
ABC				14.7					
Grand	Jan-90		15	25					Dec-90
NBC			17.6	14.6					
Wings	Apr-90				19		18		?
NBC					14.6		13.9		
Seinfeld	May-90					25	3	1	?
NBC						13.7	19.4	20.6	
Evening Shade	Sep-90				15	19			May-94
CBS					15.6	14.5			
Fresh Prince/	Sep-90				22	16	21		?
Bel Air / NBC					14.3	14.6	13.7		
Home Improvement	Sep-91				4	3	2	3	?
ABC					17.5	19.4	20.4	19.5	
Room for Two	Mar-92				10				Jul-93
ABC					16.7				
Love and War	Sep-92					15	13		Feb-95
CBS						14.7	14.5		
Hangin' with Mr.	Sep-92					16			?
Coop / ABC						14.6			
Hearts Afire	Sep-92					20			Feb-95
CBS						14.3			

	Start	1988–89	1989–90	1990–91	1991–92	1992–93	1993–94	1994–95	End
Mad about You	Sep-92							11	?
NBC								15.2	
Jackie Thomas	Dec-92					16			Mar-93
ABC						14.6			
Grace Under Fire	Sep-93						5	4	?
ABC							17.7	18.6	
Frasier	Sep-93						7	15	?
NBC							16.8	14.5	
Dave's World	Sep-93						21	21	?
CBS							13.7	12.9	
The Nanny	Nov-93							24	?
CBS								12.5	
Ellen	Mar-94							13	?
ABC								14.8	
Friends	Sep-94							8	?
NBC								15.6	
Madman of the Peop	Sep-94							12	Jun-95
NBC								14.9	
Me and the Boys	Sep-94							20	?
ABC								13.1	
Cybill	Jan-95							22	?
CBS								12.8	
Hope and Gloria	Mar-95							14	?
ABC								14.6	

television; thus, he asserts that the "sitcom focuses the resistance" to work, education, and seriousness, thus neatly complementing the medium as a whole. Marc also claims that comedy is the core to the medium. Quoting Gilbert Seldes, he writes, "'[C]omedy is the axis on which broadcasting revolves.'"[20] Like Curtis, he notes that the centrality of the genre is shown by how much comedy pervades even serious programming and, also like Curtis, points out that the news is "happy-talk" formatted (p. 8). Moreover, "television is America's jester" (p. 7).

A different specificity argument comes from Lauren Rabinovitz, and it is not an ontological claim as much as a de facto assertion based on the way things have historically developed. Drawing from the work of Lynne Joyrich, Rabinovitz describes contemporary U.S. commercial television as aimed at women: "[A]ll viewers [are positioned] as idealized female spectators and susceptible consumers."[21] While television may not have an ontological nature directed toward women, U.S. commercial television is so directed because of assumptions about who spends the money in the household and whom the advertisers on this commercial medium wish to reach. The preferred spectator is one who will be susceptible to the advertising and able to make household purchasing decisions—hence, the focus on women (and ones of a particular age bracket). Given this de facto aspect to U.S. television, then, Rabinovitz argues with Joyrich that melodrama is the obvious preferred genre for the medium. Where does the sitcom come in? According to Rabinovitz, the U.S. commercial sitcom has a strong melodramatic and feminist slant: "If, as Joyrich argues, melodrama is the preferred television aesthetic form and the 'feminine' its pervasive spectatorial address, then the sitcom as TV's dominant fictional category becomes an especially plentiful site for such address" (p. 5). U.S. sitcoms are not "classifiably 'comic'"; they are character and relation oriented. Rabinovitz's thesis then is a classic media specificity argument: since U.S. commercial television is aimed at women, the sitcom it has produced has been shaped to fulfill an address preferred by women—and we are into a loop of success for the sitcom.[22]

Rabinovitz's thesis is based on very historical factors, moving it away from the more ahistorical theses of Curtis and Marc. It is near to the second explanation for the success of sitcoms, which is that sitcoms respond to current social conditions or transformations. A rich literature exists asserting this explanation as to the genre's popularity—especially since TV's production time is so flexibly short in relation to contemporary events. For example, Curtis quotes Norman Lear as arguing that the sitcom functions in an avant-garde role for social change. As the liberal creator of *All in the Family*, Lear has a very optimistic analysis of the success of controversial social issues sitcoms, and like others considers the sitcom particularly available to raise topics in a nonthreatening but progressive discourse.[23] John Fiske agrees in part with this position, but cautions against seeing television (and its programs) as the cause of change. Rather Fiske believes that "television is part of this movement" of changing ideological values.[24]

Fiske identifies television as the fellow traveler of progressive social change, but others view it as a conservative. Darrell Hamamoto theorizes that the TV sitcom is ideologically conflicted, but ultimately supportive of the status quo; what explains the enduring popularity of the sitcom is

(1) its multivalent social ideologies and mores that function within the larger framework of liberal democratic ideology and (2) the commercial system that produces and distributes the product for private profit alone. The former characteristic has tended toward emancipation, the latter, repression.[25]

While the sitcom has raised important social issues, the form and its discourse close down radical outcomes, preferring instead solutions in "the private sphere organized around domestic life"—"individualized and private approaches" typical of a "liberal democratic ideology" (pp. 2–3). Although looking at a different set of discourses within the sitcom, Rabinovitz comes to the same conclusion that the location of the sitcom on commercial television provides a contradictory environment that has potential for progressivist discourses but is unable eventually to permit radical solutions to the problems posed within the narrative conflicts.[26]

Other writers conclude more simply that the successful sitcom (and by extension the genre as a whole) is one that fits with the social temperament. This is the traditional "zeitgeist" or "reflection" thesis. Todd Gitlin writes of the success of the 1970s "relevant sitcoms" that "the quasi-family workplace [in *The Mary Tyler Moore Show*] therefore not only matched a new cultural mood, and met the formal requirements of a successful sitcom, it also rushed into a vacuum."[27] He further claims: "The successful shows found ways to enshrine, confirm, finally to soothe even acute psychological conflicts: the ones that inhabit the same breast" (p. 218).[28]

The success of the TV sitcom may be due to factors of media specificity or to some flexible relation to social and cultural requirements, but the explanation may be more fundamental—TV sitcoms provide pleasure. This is a third explanation for their success. TV sitcoms as a type of comedy, humor, or joking process certainly yield experiences that both sociological and psychological theories attempt to understand. I shall not review the numerous discussions about these dynamics which range, as do the discussions of sitcoms within society, from theories of viewer superiority or identification with the characters to theses of spectator resistance or containment.[29] Instead I will focus on a couple of more specific applications to television sitcoms.

One such application is Curtis's thesis that the structure of these programs provides a central position for an audience to consider transgressive opinions while still remaining in a safe location. This does not mean, according to Curtis, that individuals do not temporarily or even permanently align with the transgressive or status quo; rather, the texts themselves offer a wide range of opinions for possible agreement without ultimately requiring a viewer to line up with one side. He writes,

The "centrality" of the audience position is manifestly one of the satisfactions of watching sitcom—a position of control as a sort of guardian of the values and structures which are being transgressed. It also offers a common sense position for constructing the marginal or "extreme" in terms of age, masculinity, femininity, class and so on, as laughable. It may be that very few viewers fill that central position and that readings of sitcom can vary widely in reading the text in favour of some characters over others, but the extent to which a negotiated or oppositional position can be adopted to comedy is problematic.[30]

Curtis's notion of "control" is important: his theory permits the viewer a position of power in interpreting the materials in the text, and it is this power over meaning that is pleasurable. Such a power can extend to a speculation that other viewers also watching the show are a part of a community of spectatorship with the empowered viewer. For instance, the audience is a group that may have a "'private argot' and catch-phrases which can be 'shared'"—like "soup Nazi." The audience members are also the "arbiters" of the jokes (p. 11). Fiske puts it succinctly: what gives pleasure to TV viewers is "the pleasure in the process of making meanings, that is, over and above any pleasure in the meanings that are made."[31] The pleasure-in-meaning-making thesis has great potential for understanding what is at stake for ratings busters, and I shall return to it below.

Another application of the more general theory of pleasure in the comic for the TV sitcom comes from Mark Crispin Miller. Miller takes a less broad approach than Curtis by confining his proposition to only some viewers of U.S. network TV. Miller claims that the pleasure of the sitcom isn't universal; rather "TV is pervasively ironic, forever flattering the viewer with a sense of his/her own enlightenment. Even at its most self-important, TV is also charged with this seductive irony."[32] Moreover, the primary targets of this flattery appeal are women consumers and kids as well as any dads who do not presume to act like fathers (pp. 201–6). Miller's analysis of the position offered the viewer is much more cynical than the Curtis/Fiske thesis since Miller couches the language in terms of irony and false flattery while the Curtis/Fiske view writes of "power," "self-knowledge," and "community."

One final application of theories of pleasure to the TV sitcom that deserves special note is a somewhat offhand remark by Patricia Mellencamp in her study of *I Love Lucy*. Mellencamp suggests that what provokes pleasure in the sitcoms she is studying is related not to narrative drives and resolutions but to the performance of the actors. What constitutes "currencies of audience exchange" are "comic comparison and expectation of pleasurable performance."[33] This proposition can fit into the "pleasure-in-meaning-making" view although its focus is in a different place from where meaning is being made. In fact, as I shall show, one of the most significant features to the publicly stated reception of *The Cosby Show* was pleasure in watching Bill Cosby's antics.

These various applications of theories of pleasure from the comedic narrative and performance are quite suggestive in explaining why sitcoms are so successful in prime-time television. Economic/social theses also exist, and will constitute the last of these sets of explanatory hypotheses. Mimi White suggests that acceptable novelty is very important in attracting viewership.[34] Certainly the innovative aspects of a program can interest initial audiences, and what has been perceived as "new" about the ratings-buster sitcoms will be important in accounting for their success.

Additionally, though, U.S. network television seems to function by building and holding viewer loyalties to programs. Whether this is in fact the case needs investigation, for while ratings tell us much about numbers, they do not inform us about individuals and their behaviors. Collectively, many women between the ages of twenty-four and forty-nine may watch a program, but are they the same women week after week? Possibly, but no studies that I know of provide such information.[35]

Given that, however, the hypothesis that viewer loyalty is important for the success of any highly rated program does make common sense. While some programs immediately secure that attachment, other programs require time and, executives might claim, a lot of fooling with scheduling. Sitcoms have advantages in this process over other genres. For one thing, they are cheap to produce. Sitcoms often use very minimal sets and technical requirements. Moreover, their half-hour length requires a lesser scheduling commitment than do hour-long programs, although some evidence exists that viewers tune in to "comedy blocks" rather than to a specific show.

Additionally, sitcoms traditionally aren't violent; they offer less potentially volatile material in early prime time than do other genres such as westerns, cop shows, and family dramas. Marc argues that "the aim of television is to be normal"; "the industry is obsessed with the problem of norms, and this manifests itself in both process and product."[36] The Nielsens and demographics look to "the perimeters of objectionability and attraction," seeking a "demography democracy" (p. 6). To reach certain ratings, several audiences must be served and other audiences should not be alienated. Certainly this is the case. Thus, while some sitcoms may broaden the scope of objectionability, attracting an audience through their daring, they do so in less graphic ways than dramatic shows which may turn for their attractions to violence or visual sexual display (the rear end of Jimmy Smits or Ricky Schroeder). *All in the Family* is an interesting border case in this regard since its fame was built on breaching the edge through verbal rather than visual means. *South Park* provides a current illustration of the combination of verbal and visual taboo breaking, albeit aimed at a particular audience and (predictably) distributed through a nonnetwork channel.

It may be that because of their economic and content advantages for network operations, sitcoms are more likely to be tried out and permitted to play longer than other program genres. Hence, the overall rate of success of sitcoms is due to their greater access to network time and play, which allows the building of viewer attention and loyalty. This economic/ social explanation has sufficient merit to be included in the set of explanations for why sitcoms are so successful.

None of these four sets of explanations, however, can explain the high ratings of a very few sitcoms, ratings that are significantly stronger than the programs' near competitors. Demographic democracy aside, what makes so many people tune in? To explain blockbuster sitcoms, other explanations must be considered.

Lubricating the Social Environment

Crucial to the explanation of ratings busters is an understanding common in cultural studies today: texts are always polysemic (people can read and experience a text in very individual ways). Linguistic, semiotic, and even cognitive theories of viewers' practices of making meaning suggest that philosophical and historical conditions result in a variety of readings of any text at the same time owing to the diversity of subjects interpreting that text and the plenitude of contexts in which those readings occur. Some analysts of television argue that such a polysemy is fortunate and perhaps even exploited by commercial network television. Gitlin writes,

> If the messages are susceptible to divergent interpretations, that is no failure for television. On the contrary, a show that couldn't be interpreted variously would slide into what Larry Gelbart calls "electronic pamphleteering," whose left-liberal form is the archetypical violation of television conventions. (Right-wing shows like *The FBI*, though, could get special exemption.) This taboo unites virtually the entire industry, even most critics and the regular audience. The so-called creative community shares with network executives the desire to entertain the maximum audience; the tension usually comes when writers come up with racier, riskier, more idiosyncratic ideas of *how* to do it.[37]

This desire for "the maximum audience" isn't simple egotism; it is a prerequisite for commercial success—as long as the maximum audience includes the commercially desired demographics.

Beyond the given of polysemy, however, are broader social and psychological theories of the functions of media in our lives. As suggested in the pleasure-in-meaning-making thesis, the ability to use information for personal interchange is a fundamental activity and likely a necessity for the social human. Fiske remarks that research indicates "how common it is for television to be used as something to talk about, whether at the factory tea break, or the suburban coffee morning, or in the schoolyard."[38] Talk is important "in constructing social relations and thus our sense of social identity" (p. 78). Thus, the pleasure-in-meaning-making is not an isolated act of hubris by a viewer but critical in social and psychological survival. Of course, television programs are not the only object for such talk. Movies, sports, news events, musical groups, and so forth also enable a minimally threatening personal intercourse. This apparent leisure talk also has further advantages: it lubricates business communication.

The significance and value of such talk for developing viewer interest and loyalty are shown by the massive attention entertainment firms are giving to constructing sites on the Internet for individuals to learn more about their textual interests, communicate with others also interested in the same program, and collect memorabilia in the form of images and sounds which can be downloaded to one's own personal computer. The recent practice of networks, cable channels, and movie firms of investing significant funds into forming fan chat rooms and program web pages attests to the companies' recognition that socialization among people interested in a program or film promotes viewer loyalty and potential widening of the audience if the chat room and fan materials prove enticing.

As I shall suggest, not all the high ratings of the four sitcoms are easily pegged as food for talk at the office or grocery store the next day, but several are. Certainly, though, this social function is significant for programs that are culturally well known, even if their ratings may not have ended up with the sharp peak of the four ratings busters. Very popular programs such as *M*A*S*H*, *The Mary Tyler Moore Show*, *Cheers*, *The Simpsons*, and *Seinfeld*—just as much as many soap operas and sports events—contribute to U.S. cultural history through their traces in the daily lives of their viewers. We have significant anecdotal evidence that programs such as *Father Knows Best*—which only once made it into a year's top ten list—contributed to the archetypical image of an era.[39]

Doing much of the work of creating these traces, however, is the *public* construction of these programs as the programs for daily talk (or for maintenance in our cultural memory). The project of this book is to correlate public attention to these programs with the development of their unusually high ratings. While an absolutely precise mathematical connection will not be possible because of the lack of data and the contingencies of human behavior, I will be able suggest that as critical or public attention escalates around these programs, their ratings increase, and as their ratings increase so does talk about them. The cooperative dynamic stimulates the must-see phenomenon. Thus, to participate in daily conversation requires knowledge of the program. In short, surrogate consumers in the medium of public discourse create a cultural currency for these programs, helping other viewers "see" what might be available in the series for their enjoyment.

The focus of public discussions differs among the programs (and even among commentators for an individual series). In each case, the program has particular qualities that provide the stimulus for discussion, but the differences between the series produce very different descriptions and pleasures for their viewers. No single characteristic of a sitcom can be pulled out to insure success. For that reason, although I will engage in some textual analysis of each series, the procedures and focus of my textual study will be determined by the public discourse.

Not only can no specific textual characteristic be isolated, but neither can any particular connection to context insure fame. Some of the qualities public discourse perceives as worthy of discussion may connect to contemporary social life, but it is not the case that a perfect match between contemporary social life and the program is necessary for the ratings phenomenon to exist. For instance, while *All in the Family* certainly operated as part of a public discussion about U.S. politics and cultural change, discourse around *Laverne & Shirley* was only tangentially connected to the current social environment. While one might argue for an unconscious relation between the program and its context, such a symptomatic reading of the public discourse is less credible than accepting the proposition that not all fictional texts are directly accountable to their historical conditions. Here I would use the public discourse around the Superbowl as my proof. The high ratings for the Superbowl game are a function of the massive public discourse and "buildup" before this media event. But the Superbowl is not specifically tied to the date of its existence. Hype and high ratings existed in 1980 as much as in 1998; the meaning of the Superbowl is not particularly altered by its date. Sitcoms operate equally semi-autonomously. While it is probably the case that a program seriously out of step with the needs of individuals within a social formation could not be successful, entertainment seems to function according to long-standing social and psychological dynamics beyond the contingencies of the immediate day. Programs seem to work, in fact, *because of* their distance. All that can be generalized is that in order for a sitcom to become a blockbuster, public attention must reach such a level as to intrigue the right consumers to watch enough episodes to become faithful viewers.

Thus, to account for the exceptionally high ratings of just four sitcoms during the course of U.S. prime-time television, the following must be considered: the polysemic nature of texts; the aesthetic, psychological, and sociological possibilities for pleasure; historical institutional features including the economic structure of U.S. television at the time of the blockbuster's rise; and, importantly, the role of surrogate consumers in creating cultural currency for viewers. What will follow in the four case studies are not reception studies that might explain how various sorts of individuals experienced and used these programs in their daily lives—the subject of much of my research in the past several years. Instead, I will examine how network television and public commentators as surrogate consumers have at various moments responded to broadcasting's blockbusters. It is these historical conditions for reception that provide grounding for further studies of uses of the sitcoms by groups or individuals.

What will follow will also not add up to some master narrative, although I will suggest some conclusions in the epilogue. An important feature of contemporary poststructuralist historiography is the avoidance of grand stories. I do not think it is theoretically appropriate to tie the success of these four programs to some general thesis about these programs and culture as a whole. Such a thesis might be that popular culture helps viewers work through their personal needs. However, none of the evidence supports generalization to individuals or individuals within a social formation. Rather it is important to realize that television is a very particular form of cultural transmission: its constant flow of programming and its potential for transmitting images of live events contribute to its media specificity; television programs are not necessarily an example of "popular" culture since they serve the interests of advertisers, networks, and producers (the long-standing adage that television sells audiences to advertisers); for various blockbuster programs, different groups of people were more inclined than others to watch; television is by no means "the popular medium" until we define who constitutes the group that uses "popular" culture and how many of those people consider TV as providing them with "their" culture. Thus, my argument and theoretical position would be compromised if I tried to explain these programs under some general proposition about culture. What I do hope to accomplish is several detailed historical and textual studies of programs that did consistently capture more members of the TV audience than just the normal fare.

[2]

The Beverly Hillbillies

In May 1961 Federal Communications Commission Chairman Newton N. Minow attacked television as "a vast wasteland." In September 1962, *The Beverly Hillbillies* premiered on CBS, almost as proof of Minow's assertion. If, however, Minow was correct, by the end of the season, 36 percent of all television homes in the United States were regularly tuned in to a program that the *New York Times* critic initially called "strained and unfunny," working with a "broad premise . . . followed by a succession of events too absurd to be even slightly amusing."[1] If a cultural elite critic thought that, so did one of the industry trade papers. *Variety* perceived *The Beverly Hillbillies* as an imitation of the six-year-old *The Real McCoys*, in the same vein of "corn" and rural comedy developed at ABC. Moreover, the program was "painful to sit through," "improbable and impossible as the characters who people it." The reviewer thought the "lines were as cliché-ridden as the situations were obvious."[2]

Reviews by *Time, Newsweek,* and the *New York Times* during the first month of *The Beverly Hillbillies'* broadcasting hardly improved. *Time* described *The Beverly Hillbillies* by recounting a couple of its jokes and subtitling a picture of the family as "hogs in a better corn." *Newsweek* considered the program as having an "odd" set of heroes.[3] Jack Gould of the *New York Times* told his readers to relax: the "heady cultural ferment" that seemed to start the fall was calming to a slight breeze. Thirty million Americans had found a new hit: *The Beverly Hillbillies*—already in fourth place behind *Lucille Ball, Andy Griffith,* and *Danny Thomas.* He continued:

The in-group outside TV obviously overlooked the basic hunger of the country in artistic matters: Ozark humor. "Beverly Hillbillys" [*sic*] is steeped in enough twanging guitar, polkadot gingham, deliberative drawl, prolific cousins and rural no-think to make each half hour seem as if it contained 60 minutes.[4]

Additional descriptions included "hayseed wholesomeness" and "they do not merely strain credulity; they crush it."

The problem for these reviewers was that the program confronted the cultural elite's notions of quality entertainment. As the ratings remained high, *Time* devoted an additional article in late November to *The Beverly Hillbillies.* The essay's tenor, however, began to shift slightly. While the program was described as "dedicated to finding out how many times the same joke can be repeated," the writer also took up the spirit by starting the review: "The pone is the lowest form of humor." Now the characters were "nicely played" and "engaging people." The conclusion: "[T]he show is supplying an apparent demand for straightforward, unsophisticated, skill-fully performed humor. 'It's my kind of corn,' says Director [Richard] Whorf—'right on the cob.'"[5]

Indeed, it was not realism that *The Beverly Hillbillies* seemed to present to its first critics. Nor was its plot very complicated or intellectual. The trouble seemed to be its obviousness. An excessively transparent television.

Newsweek agreed at just about the same time. It too seemed to want to account for a program that was beating major competitors, even if the other shows were no more what Minow was seeking than was *The Beverly Hillbillies.* *Hillbillies* had started the season with a 28 rating. By its second week it had climbed to 31.3, fourth behind *Lucille Ball* at 34.8. Second was *Andy Griffith* (32.8); third was *Danny Thomas* (32.5). *Bonanza* came in tied with *The Beverly Hillbillies.* By the fourth week of the season, *The Beverly Hillbillies* was up to 33.7. Second place went to *Lucille Ball* at 30.9, some 2.8 points lower, with *Ben Casey* and *Bonanza* close to *Ball.* The situation continued through the fall. Nielsens ending for 23 December gave *The Beverly Hillbillies* first place at 33.2; *Candid Camera* came in second at 33.1; *Gunsmoke* was third at 29.1.

Newsweek, like *Time*, tried to figure this out. Titling its review essay "The Corn Is Green," the writer declared the program "the most shamelessly corny show in years" and "triumphant foolishness." The writer quoted producer Paul Henning as boasting, "It's not cerebral. There's no message except 'have fun.'"[6]

What had happened so far is important. First of all, the program was being described as exceptionally formulaic. No writer so far could figure out anything new about *The Beverly*

Hillbillies—except perhaps the excessiveness with which it reproduced dumb jokes. Secondly, the writers were clearly characterizing the program as low art. With its fondness for puns and "unsophisticated" humor, it was being described as requiring no intellectual effort.

The program at this point, moreover, would not qualify as a blockbuster hit. While number one in ratings, its second place competitor was right on its heels. Yet by the end of the season, *The Beverly Hillbillies* secured a 36.0 average rating, while *Candid Camera* ended up tied with *Red Skelton*, both at 31.1, some 4.9 points off *Hillbillies*. What happened?

It appears to me that important events in redefining the cultural currency of *The Beverly Hillbillies* were essays published in the 15 December issue of *TV Guide* and the 5 January copy of *Saturday Review*.[7] Written by Gilbert Seldes, dean of promoting popular culture, the *TV Guide* essay provided two useful strategies for approving the program as acceptable TV fare. Seldes argued: (1) *The Beverly Hillbillies* can be compared with other great American classics of comedy; and (2) a variation from the rural comedy formula does exist in the program. Seldes began his essay:

The thumping success of *The Beverly Hillbillies* has already sent some serious thinkers to the wailing wall, and when you tune the program in, you are supposed to ask yourself, "What is America coming to?" As I am still laughing, I think back to the days when custard pies and Keystone Cops were flying through the air [*sic*], and a lot of people were convinced America was a cultural "desert"—the 1920 word for "wasteland."[8]

Seldes then invoked Charlie Chaplin. He also argued that while the usual formula for comedy was "'real people in unreal situations.' Here you have unreal people in unreal situations."

Robert Lewis Shayon for the *Saturday Review* added a third strategy for higher-brow interpretation: the comedy was actually disguised as social satire. This was "situation-farce." "Comedy, as we know, is a weapon with which society socializes inferiors." Each week the Clampetts attack our values and "standards"—specifically, "our money-oriented value system," but we return, hoping they will be socialized to our norms. "The horror experienced by the neighbors [of the Clampetts] is ours. The standards of the Clampetts are heretical. They cannot be endured because they require that we re-examine our own standards and discover their hollowness." To have "valid social criticism with a top-ten Nielsen is an absolute rarity in television. This is the true measure of the success of 'Beverly Hillbillies'—first of its kind."[9] Thus, the *Saturday Review* essay not only again suggested "highbrow" possibilities for the program, but also marked it as different, as new, and perhaps even as a critique of "highbrowism."

Within a month, the *Saturday Evening Post* devoted a multipage article and cover issue to *The Beverly Hillbillies*. The picture was a takeoff of Grant Wood's *American Gothic,* with Jed Clampett holding a pitchfork, Granny beside him. Although mostly an essay about the program's production background and how Filmways created a major publicity apparatus with massive tie-ins and merchandising, the author did quote members of the production company comparing *The Beverly Hillbillies* to the comedy of Chaplin and Harold Lloyd. Marty Ransohoff, board chairman of Filmways: "'Everyone who went to see Harold Lloyd or Charlie Chaplin

felt as though the schnook they were watching was much further in the doghouse than they were.'"[10] Although I personally cannot see the analogy working—I remember wishing I
were as "bad off" as the Clampetts—the allusion to masters

of comedy is more significant. Thus, *The Beverly Hillbillies* was being positioned as resistant to the highbrow cultural elitism of Newton Minow as well as invoking the classic American rube-fool as wise man figure. Critical discourse was constructing the program as *popular*, as of the American people. Such an ideological gesture fit well into the landscape of early 1960s American culture attitudes and network television agendas. Both some consumer surrogates and TV executives could turn to *The Beverly Hillbillies* and declare it exemplified what were core values for America. Other viewers, of course, could continue to enjoy the program not as satire but as corn.[11]

Mass Culture and the Egghead

Recent scholarship on the 1950s and 1960s has emphasized that demarcations between cultural levels shifted toward the end of the 1950s as individuals began to question earlier assumptions about the effects of mass media. These mass culture debates, while certainly not apparent in the direct discussions of *The Beverly Hillbillies*, underlay Gould's and then other writers' evaluations of the program. Although the rise of mass printings of paperback books, cinema, and radio aroused public concerns, these concerns took on a new appearance when television arrived after World War II. The number of television sets was less than one million in 1949, but the next decade saw that number explode to 46 million by 1960; 90 percent of American homes had TV, and the families were watching it on an average of five hours per day.[12]

Mass media provoked mixed views among public intellectuals, and this is evident in papers published in 1959 from a symposium on the subject, "Problems of Mass Culture and Mass Media," sponsored by *Daedalus* and the Taminment Institute of New York City. Entitled *Culture for the Millions?*, the conference proceedings rehearsed the ambivalences about culture and media circulating at this point. Editor Norman Jacobs noted that the symposium's speakers seemed most concerned about "middlebrow" culture, presumably experienced in large part from television although also permeating culture through book-of-the-month clubs, music, and glossy Hollywood movie spectacles. Thus, some participants in the symposium argued that "people in mass society have lost the ability to take cultural issues seriously."[13] A version of the Frankfurt School/Adorno/Horkheimer thesis, the view here is that middle-class tastes neither require the exercise of individual thinking stimulated by highbrow culture nor display the naturalness of folk art, the culture of the people (apparent in "lowbrow culture"). Theodor Adorno and Max Horkheimer in their essay "The Culture Industry" praised the nonsense of comedians such as Chaplin and the Marx Brothers for toppling artificial mediocrity;[14] intellectuals of the 1950s also found such absurdist wit to be far superior to the contrivances of formulaic comedy. Thus, the concern of these intellectuals was the drabness of response. Reactions that were real, either real thought or real resistances to the norms, were better. Leo Rosten, a conference participant who was then writing for *Look* magazine, declared:

A great deal of what appears in the mass media is dreadful tripe and treacle; inane in content, banal in style, muddy in reasoning, mawkish in sentiment, vulgar, naive, and offensive to men of learning or refinement. I am both depressed and distressed by the bombardment of our eyes, our ears, and our brains by meretricious material designed for a populace whose paramount preferences involve the narcotic pursuit of "fun."[15]

However, Rosten went on to remark that the intelligentsia are sometimes slow to—but they do—acknowledge talent in the popular arts. The Marx Brothers, for example, are now "the eggheads' delight" (p. 77).

The reasons for this ambivalence, as Andrew Ross has detailed, relate to Cold War politics. Tracing debates about taste cultures beginning with Clement Greenberg's 1939 "Avant Garde and Kitsch" essay, Ross notes that post–World War II intellectuals initially considered mass culture as a virus, much like communism.[16] Avoiding brainwashing, curing undetectable diseases, and defusing the threat of a populace unable to protect itself from propaganda were the goals of cultural guardians. However, this rhetoric could also transform into a description of American culture as "mass," or worse, no better than the culture of fascist Germany or the socialist Soviet Union. It was better, as Ross points out, to reconsider Americans and *their* mass culture as creating not mindless conformity but, at least in the case of *The Beverly Hillbillies*, adept social criticism which promoted individuality.

Ross argues that two protective solutions developed for justifying U.S. mass culture. One was the "frustrated or disappointed, aesthetic-liberal position" (p. 54): people prefer middlebrow culture, and, after all is said and done, America is a democracy. We need to respect the people's choices. The second was the "corporate-liberal or progressive evolutionist position." Middlebrow culture really isn't that bad; it is actually "benign," serving as training for consumption and as therapeutic for the populace. As Ross lays this out, the aesthetic-liberal position divorces middle-class culture from its industrial sources, while the corporate-liberal position comprehends middle-class culture as functional for consumer capitalism. The aesthetic-liberal view defines preferences as "natural"; the corporate-liberal view focuses on their potential social function. The outcome of the aesthetic-liberal attitude would be a laissez-faire distancing from cultural production, but the corporate-liberal might see advantages in directing or educating the people's choices. The corporate-liberal position, in its more aggressive mode, could take on the character of paternalism or at least a much more directed agenda for organizing culture for its middle-class consumers.

Both of these liberal positions existed in the discourse of the symposium recorded in *Culture for the Millions?* An important and prescient statement of the corporate-liberal position occurred in the paper presented by Arthur Schlesinger, Jr., "Notes on a National Cultural Policy."[17] Schlesinger called for standards in such national media as television and radio to counter a rising ordinariness. Specifically, he suggested finding a way to equalize "the alleged competitive disadvantages of enlightened programing" (p. 149) by policy making, including creating a minimum number of hours of cultural and educational programming and allocating control of content to the networks (rather than advertisers). Stations should be reviewed annually, and a "revitalization of the FCC [Federal Communications Commission]" should occur. Schlesinger noted that "Walter Lippmann and others have recently argued for the establishment of a public network" (p. 151), and the government should consider a Federal Council on Arts to stimulate and support (high) art. Schlesinger's list of proposals fit both a highbrow and corporate-liberal ideology, and prepared the path for Minow's term as FCC chair.

Thus, the period in which *The Beverly Hillbillies* arrived was not a time of unified liberal opinion about the possible values of television mass entertainment. A swing away from a rigid rejection of mass-produced culture derived from needs to promote differences from other "mass" societies and to create advantages for an extremely profitable product. Ambivalence and contradictory interpretations of the meanings and effects of mass media existed among cultural commentators in the late 1950s and early 1960s. Examples to prove either the degradation of taste or the free expression of popular individuality could be created for arguing a specific reading of the output of network television. It is important to note that Ross labels both the aesthetic-liberal and the corporate-liberal views as "liberal." Indeed, both positions were "hands-off" television, opposing direct control of content through censorship; however, the corporate-liberal view was not opposed to adjusting regulatory dynamics to increase the opportunity for less competitive goods to contend successfully in the marketplace of ideas.

The Television Industry and the Vast Wasteland

The concern of these liberal intellectuals was not only to widen good taste and thereby produce an intelligent public but also to guarantee national security. As Michael Curtin discusses in *Redeeming the Wasteland*, Minow, and others like him, believed the U.S. position in the Cold War could be easily undermined by a stupefied public. Curtin writes that for these individuals, "Americans [were] lazy and insular. In their eyes, average Americans lacked a sense of purpose and resolve, both of which would be necessary if the United States was to meet the challenge from the East."[18] The success of the Soviets' publicity coup in launching the Sputnik in 1957 created a crisis in public education. What better way, these U.S. leaders thought, to turn around American self-complacency than to utilize the public airwaves as they should be used—for public good.

While Minow's "vast wasteland" speech shook up the industry and became a touchstone for the Kennedy administration's mass media policy—despite the fact that, as Minow remarked, he used the phrase only once in his address to the National Association of Broadcasters (NAB)—what was coming was succinctly forecast in the hearings over Minow's appointment. At that time, he stated that the role of the FCC included "elevating and encouraging better television programs. Since I believed television was underestimating the taste level of the American public, I expressed the hope that we could have 'more open spaces between the Westerns and more public affairs than private eyes.'"[19] Even at the hearings, he declared that the "airwaves belong to the people," and that at license renewal time, stations would be checked closely.

Minow's May 1961 "inaugural" address to the NAB began with some reassurances: most specifically that the FCC would not censor the stations. But then Minow came down hard on prime-time content. Of the 73 1/2 hours of major-time broad-casting, 59 had been devoted to "action-adventure, situation comedy, variety, quiz and movies" (p. 52). In often quoted lines, Minow declaims:

But when television is bad, nothing is worse. . . . I can assure you that you will observe a vast waste-land.

You will see a procession of game shows, violence, audience participation shows, formula comedies about totally unbelievable families, blood and thunder, mayhem, violence, sadism, murder, Western badmen, Western good men, private eyes, gangsters, more violence, and cartoons. And, endlessly, commercials—many screaming, cajoling and offending. And most of all, boredom. (P. 52)

Curtin and other historians such as Eric Barnouw [20] note that this speech and its general policy implications for the Kennedy administration underlined what the networks and NAB had already concluded as a consequence of the recent quiz show scandals: they had better clean up their store, or at least put in a new window display.[21] These historians suggest that the flush of documentaries and public affairs programming was one of the networks' gestures that they took seriously their responsibility to the public good.

Yet another response, imbedded in that one, was resentment. Minow called not only for reducing violence in the dramatic shows but for altering the overall balance of the genres away from fiction. This was counter to the networks' estimation of what Americans wanted to watch, and what advertisers were thus interested in paying for. Specifically, at CBS, James Aubrey had recently arrived back as vice-president, with a charge to refashion the network after the quiz show scandals. Aubrey is particularly well known for his "broads, bosoms, and fun" memo in which he urged those features for CBS shows, and he was certainly out for profits first. Aubrey's "dictum" aimed to capture the youth market. Such goals for network television were at odds with Minow's.[22]

Moreover, as part of late 1950s programming trends, networks had increasingly turned from live theatrical drama produced in New York City to filmed action-adventures made in Hollywood. This literal shift in type, genre, and source of programming reproduced for Minow and his compatriots the belief that reality, realism, and high art were losing out to artificiality, fantasy, and mass entertainment. But for the broadcasters, Minow's call also portended loss of income.

Minow threatened the broadcasters not only by declaring that *content* (and thus network profits) would be an issue for his FCC but by expecting diversity in programming and programming for children. Moreover, to ensure these changes took place, license renewals would cease to be automatic and would involve real hearings. Minow noted concerns about the concentration of powerful networks and suggested that local stations would be expected to take up more responsibility for their programming choices. Minow's agenda eventually produced a requirement that all TV sets be capable of receiving UHF (thus facilitating the possibility of increasing the number of stations in local areas), the formation of a corporation for communications satellites (COMSAT, 1962), and the passage of the ETV (Educational TV) Facilities Act of 1962, which provided federal funding to match local educational station construction.

The "vast wasteland" speech attracted much public attention—both positive and critical. Senator William O. Proxmire called it "courageous and provocative."[23] Over ten thousand messages arrived at the FCC, the largest response to a public issue to that point. Highbrow commentators such as Shayon for *Saturday Review* (who would shortly find *The Beverly Hillbillies* "valid social criticism") praised Minow's speech, describing it as having "courage, candor, and integrity" but questioning whether the people cared.[24] Articles, columns, and jokes abounded. And, as I have already suggested above, Minow shortly became the oblique target of a popular rebuke to the culture standards he attempted to secure for the nation.[25]

Minow's position might best be described as a "corporate-liberal, progressive evolutionist" attitude. With adequate exposure to better fare, Americans would naturally gravitate toward better programming which, in turn, would prepare them to be better participants in democratic actions both domestically and internationally.

The broadcasting industry, however, chuckled when Americans failed to take up the opportunity that Minow created for them. For example, *Changing Times* reported for the new fall season following Minow's address:

Last May [1961], Federal Communications Commissioner Chairman Newton M. Minow made a frontal attack on TV programming and programs. "A vast wasteland" was his label for the medium. He said there was far too much violence, formula comedy, blood and thunder, western badmen, mayhem and murder. Smarting under the accusation, the TV industry denied the charge and invited the public to judge for itself. Here's what the 1961–62 season will offer.

In brief: Sponsors will stick to the proven formula of westerns, action-adventure, comedy. There will be more of the latter two, somewhat fewer in the western category. Innovation will be sparse. . . . Four out of five programs will have more than one sponsor.[26]

Over 80 percent of prime-time shows would be filmed or taped. In the years to follow, CBS's strategy paid off. In 1963, with *The Beverly Hillbillies* as its lead program, CBS led the other two networks, bringing in 39 percent of the total revenues against NBC's 35 percent and ABC's 26 percent.[27]

During the twenty-eight-month tenure of Minow as FCC chair, broadcasters and pundits habitually used the "vast wasteland" accusation as either a rallying cry for regulation of content or the sign of a bureaucrat out of touch with the public. One way out of the impasse, as I have suggested, is to cast the wasteland as misinterpreted. Particularly in the case of comedy, this could be accomplished by a polysemic gesture: yes, the program may look formulaic, but beneath its surface is American social commentary. Moreover, the values that the program promotes are traditional American values, ones desirable in the era of the "New Frontier." Such a transformative gesture actually benefits both liberals (of either ilk) and industry personnel. Redesigning the meaning of a popular program permits the possibility of making everyone happy.

Reading the Corn

Unfortunately, data from the Nielsens are extremely hard to obtain, and, moreover, in the early 1960s, public presentations of the Nielsens categorized viewers solely by house-holds.[28] It would be one of those golden moments of scholar-ship if I were able to show that as soon as several middle- to highbrow commentators justified *The Beverly Hillbillies* as social criticism, not only did a rise in viewership occur (which I have already presented), but demographics alter to include people more likely to adhere to highbrow tastes. But I can't present such data. Moreover, I am not particularly inclined to think that that necessarily is what did happen. Rather, I think that, at most, the creation of a reading strategy invoking "so-cial criticism" simply eased the decision not to turn away from the channel that provided another comedy focusing on rural characters.

Thus, what the redefinition of *The Beverly Hillbillies* prob-ably accomplished was a relaxation of any middle-class guilt. The viewer wasn't stooping to low- or middlebrow fare but rising to the heady realms of satire. Encouraged by analogies to Chaplin and Lloyd (if not the Marx Brothers and the Key-stone Cops) and by multiply occurring public linkages to Al Capp's social and political vitriol in the comic strip *Dogpatch, U.S.A.* (Nielsen) families would not have to hide their viewing choice.[29] Americans would not be such dolts as to watch a wasteland.

Other scholars have speculated about what early 1960s au-diences might have gathered and used from *The Beverly Hill-billies*. In particular, David Marc is one of the writers most at-tentive to this genre. In his *Comic Visions* (1989), he is fairly pessimistic, writing that "shows as *The Beverly Hillbillies* and *Gilligan's Island* [1964–1967] seemed utterly indifferent to verisimilitude, preferring instead to explore and allegorize the turgid daydreams of American mass culture."[30] However, in his earlier *Demographic Vistas* (1984), he shows more complexity in his analysis of the series. Describing *The Beverly Hillbillies* as a break from the domestic comedies of the 1950s in which a child's crisis propels events, Marc writes that the program "invites the viewer into the epic arena of testing cultural assumptions."[31]

Donna McCrohan and Paul Attallah, like Marc, agree that, if you want to read *The Beverly Hillbillies* as social satire, then the satire focuses on culture, tastes, and consumption. As I shall reinforce below, their readings correspond at least generally with what the period commentators perceived to be the targets of the wit. Moreover, as I shall emphasize, such wit expresses a populist position that ironically mocks the direction in which television is headed: to artificiality and Beverly Hills/Hollywood. Such a twist of messages is scarcely a problem for television producers (and Hollywood moguls) who are quite ready to gather in the bucks no matter how they might reach the cash box.

Although Marc, McCrohan, and Attallah agree that the comedy of *The Beverly Hillbillies* is directed toward cultural values as evidenced in lifestyle choices, how they construct the oppositions implied by "choice" differs. Marc organizes the dispute as between country folk ("healthy, good") and city people ("neurotic, bad") (p. 55); "the object of lampoon is modernity" (p. 62). McCrohan also suggests modernity as the general target, but she concentrates the critique as reflecting "the bewilderment of newly affluent Americans unsettled by the technological jungle."[32] The program voices the resentment felt by average people toward intellectuals, toward "city slickers" (p. 129). Likewise, Attallah believes that "social class" provides the "discursive disruption" but emphasizes that sexuality is also explored, although in a very nonthreatening manner that reinforces conservative values of gender distinctions, heterosexuality, and monogamy.[33]

Typecasting and early publicity for the show established a context for reading the program as promoting traditional America against new America. Buddy Ebsen had recently starred as Davy Crockett's sidekick in Walt Disney's *Ballad of Davy Crockett*.[34] Even in July 1962, before the first episode aired, CBS publicity described *The Beverly Hillbillies* as "farcical."[35] Then in the first weeks of the program, interviews with the stars reinforced such interpretations. In an article in the *New York Herald Tribune* dated 4 November 1962, the reporter permitted Ebsen to create a reading strategy:

"The public is hungry for what we offer—honest humor," Ebsen said. "We're friendly people, but some of our humor has a biting comment. If the show has any overtones, any message, it's that people have more than they need in this material world. Our social comment is that people should live simpler, not necessarily like the Clampetts, but simpler."[36]

This theme of anticonsumption traverses the program's reception. It certainly pervaded Shayon's January 1963 *Saturday Review* essay noted earlier as a major break from previous discussions of the show. Shayon saw the program as a "challenge to our money-oriented value system" and permitted program creator Paul Henning to declare, "Our characters will remain honest, sincere, moral, and loyal people in a setting of sophistication of modern life."[37]

Moreover, such a challenge to modern America might be embraced by the notorious tastemongers, which the highbrows were often accused of being: "The family is pure comic strip, the dialogue outrageous corn, but even highbrows find themselves laughing in spite of themselves" (p. 32). In America, taste cultures and consumption preferences *can be overridden* by our fundamental belief in core values such as honesty and integrity. This consensual reading of *The Beverly Hillbillies* offers open arms to embrace everyone, denying that class differences are anything more that consumption choices. Even people living in Beverly Hills might choose a lifestyle based on need rather than conspicuous display.

By the following season, the critical discourse on *The Beverly Hillbillies* had settled into a routine. Arnold Hano opened a November 1963 *New York Times Magazine* story on the program:

The taste of the Great American Public—hereinafter G.A.P.—has often been a source of dismay, especially to a small, self-appointed culture cult that becomes especially pained when G.A.P.'s taste differs markedly from its own. Fads such as "The Music Goes 'Round and 'Round," hula hoops, Liberace, Ma and Pa Kettle, pegged pants, Hopalong Cassidy, Davy Crockett, the Twist and Liz Taylor arouse more than irritation in this high- and middle-brow cabal. The cult would really love to do something about it all—like quick, cheap burial. Each to his own taste (the cult says it in the original French of course), but only if you can throw a picket line around the building where some of these eaches go forth to scratch.[38]

Hano continued by admitting that "the show bores me," but it was "no national disaster, nor is it necessary for us to follow David Susskind's advice and write our Congressman

(Susskind is alarmed that imitators may spring up and Hill-billy us to death)" (p. 30).

Along with repeating the themes that the program re-bukes modern complexity, snobbery, and taste hierarchies while supporting honesty and integrity, Hano constructed the comedic oppositions as a "return to nature, to natural ways" versus city-folk ways. Hano found in *The Beverly Hillbillies* "a twitting of shallowness and of pretentious-ness" (pp. 122–23). This theme had also been proposed by Lawrence Laurent in the *Los Angeles Times* in June 1963, when he explained the popularity of the program as a re-turn to what Rousseau praised: "noble savages." Quoting Rousseau, he wrote, "'What wisdom can you find that is greater than kindness?'"[39]

While not remarked upon by every commentator, a final theme of the discourse around the program was its gentleness. Perhaps if *The Beverly Hillbillies* had succumbed to the acer-bic tongue of Al Capp, highbrow advocates might have em-braced it, although whether the G.A.P. would have followed is another matter. In fact, in reviewing it today, I am struck by what the program's producers touted as its strengths: no one is hurt, no misunderstanding creates pain, and good humor abounds.

Simply sampling some of the first season's episodes reveals the soft touch of the program and its reliance on verbal play for the comedic disruption.[40] Many of the jokes do revolve around puns, but the puns are less sharp verbal wit to lacer-ate an opponent than a homey comedy derived from varied cultural perspectives. When asked by banker Milburn Drys-dale's assistant Jane Hathaway whether Jethro has been to

Eton (England), Jed responds that Jethro has "been to eaten" all right! Other jokes result from the same dynamic even when they are not puns. Told that Beverly Hills doesn't have ice or snow, the Clampetts ask if some couldn't be brought in.

Humor derives from verbal play but also from action or visual sources. In the opening episode, which is a general motivating plot of the discovery of oil on the Clampett land and Jed's decision to go to Beverly Hills for the sake of the two adolescents, Jane has announced to Mr. Drysdale that she has arranged for flamingos to be put on the grounds of the Clampetts' new Beverly Hills estate. Granny assumes they are strange chickens and tries to catch one for dinner. The bars around their home are misrecognized as cues for a prison, perhaps leading to a major motif for the early season. Is the new environment an opportunity or a restriction?

Verbal, action, and visual wit that is seldom directed against any individual, no matter how much he or she may deserve it, keeps the program from becoming cruel or controversial. Another strategy implied in the responses but never specifically addressed is the explicit reproduction of the wise father. In lumping this program with "rural comedies," critics then and more recently made the domestic situation comedy formula easy to miss. Yet part of the discourses about "naturalness" and core American values probably derived from casting Buddy Ebsen as Jed and making Jed a "father who knows best."[41]

This ploy is articulated in the second episode when Jed explains to Elly May that one reason he chose to move to Beverly Hills was that it was time for Elly May to begin growing up and acting like a girl. Taking the blame, Jed apologizes, "I raised you like a boy and I was wrong to do it. . . . It ain't fitting. It ain't right for folks to go against nature." This construction of Jed is also produced by the only significant shooting style anomaly for the program. Although at times camera angle choices are a bit awkward, the cinematography duplicates normal television practices except for occasional head shots of Jed. These close-ups are not shot at head height as they are for the other characters; rather, the camera is positioned lower than normal and tilts up to generate a slightly low-angle shot. Most of the occasions when this shot is used, Jed is posed, thinking. Sometimes Jed is merely puzzled about circumstances; at other times, he is making a decision.

While likely scarcely noticeable to any but the trained eye, the effect of this shooting choice is to focus the drama around Jed as the silent center amidst the storm of both his relatives and the Beverly Hills hucksters. Ultimately, plots don't particularly resolve themselves based on a wise decision by Jed. In fact, Attallah rightly observes that often the plots aren't resolved at all; the program just ends.[42]

Yet only rarely does Jed make a blunder. In the first episode, Jed does mistakenly believe that his home is a prison, and he counsels his family to run for the hills, with the last shots of the episode showing the group fleeing through the streets and foliage of the residences. However, in most other episodes, Jed exercises much more caution, carefully surveying the circumstances and acting as a wise giver of advice. Seldom is Jed involved in a major disturbance. For example, when a city slicker tries to sell Jed the Hollywood Bowl, Griffith Park, and the Park Zoo, the slicker throws in the freeway connecting the areas. Outraged by drivers on the road yelling at them for driving too slowly, Granny, Jethro, and Elly Mae stop the traffic and make the people promise to drive with courtesy. Jed is not involved in this error.

The discussions around *The Beverly Hillbillies* consistently focus on the wise rube, a long-standing figure in American folklore. Jed fills that role for the program and permits surrogate consumers and audiences to link it to core central U.S. values. Placing that figure in the center of an archetypical American family permits reading the show as gentle humor, a domestic sitcom, and social criticism. Readers can have it lots of way, and even if the program is an affront to eggheads, highbrow culture may not represent what is best about and for the country. No viewer sat down in front of the television and said, I am going to resist Minow and others like him. But viewers did sit down and think, I am going to enjoy some traditional American fun.

While the clash over tastes and appropriate reading strategies occupied surrogate consumers' attention, two other factors may have contributed to the success of this program: the age of the television viewer and the function of in-home media entertainment. In 1965, 41 percent of the U.S. population was nineteen years old or younger (an effect of the baby boom).[43] This population bubble was probably critical in the raw numbers for *The Beverly Hillbillies* and other comedies of the mid-1960s (and then later the ascendency of *All in the Family* as that generation moved into its early twenties). Connected to these demographics is the pleasure that nonrelevancy may have provided youthful viewers. Simultaneous with the success of *The Beverly Hillbillies* was an intensification of Cold War and civil rights struggles. In May 1960, U-2 pilot Francis

Powers was shot down over Russia. In spring 1961, Alan Shepard rode into outer space as America's entry into that territorial battle. That season also witnessed the beginning of Freedom Riders in the U.S. South. The program's premiere in November 1962 coincided with the showdown in Cuba over the potential deployment of Soviet missiles. Unquestionably, uncovering what various segments of the audience experienced in their viewing of *The Beverly Hillbillies* will contribute to understanding better the blockbuster status of this program.

Conclusion

No doubt the publicity apparatus assembled by Filmways was important in creating the first audience. According to the *Saturday Evening Post* interview, Filmways began six weeks before the start of the program and believed it had reached thirty-five million people in eighty-five cities prior to the first episode. Thus, the initial rating for *The Beverly Hillbillies* may be due to the general publicity machine.

However, the early numbers for *The Beverly Hillbillies* cannot account for the increase that occurred after December and that caused the program to end up with a rating of 36. The explanation likely is that the public discourse in major information sources interested new groups of viewers beyond the initial set, who tuned in to see what the fuss was all about. As surrogate consumers, the reviewers in *TV Guide*, the *Saturday Review*, and the *Saturday Evening Post* indicated to other subgroups that something was worth viewing here and discussing the next day. Was the program evidence of the deterioration of America or a reassurance that American core values still held us together?

Moreover, the "December" discourse set in place the two factors that I am hypothesizing as significant for blockbuster hits. The program was constructed as potentially having appeal for a second audience beyond the first one. Although all texts are polysemic, major institutional sites were indicating that *The Beverly Hillbillies* could now be read not as lowbrow humor (e.g., the rural comedy) but as social satire of interest, ironically, to some of the very highbrow audience to which Minow's remarks were addressed. Moreover, if you wanted to be in the know, you would want to see this most recent example of long-standing American naive but resistant primitivism. Appealing to the traditions of the wise fool, the Chaplins and Lloyds, the Grant Woods of American culture, our fathers-who-know-best, these several essays in middle- to upper-class magazines and newspapers authorized new program viewers to pay attention and reassured current watchers. The gentleness of the joking and the warmth of a comedic family may also have provided comfort to youthful viewers.

Privy perhaps to more information about actual viewers, the producers of *The Beverly Hillbillies* also indicated within a couple of years what they thought was continuing to produce interest in the program. Two spin-offs of *The Beverly Hillbillies* were created, both of which secured a good audience and one of which had continuing fame: *Petticoat Junction* (running from 1963 through 1970) and *Green Acres* (1965 to 1971). Like their source, these programs used culture and taste clashes to generate gentle humor while the domestic sitcom functioned as the base formula. These culture-clash, domestic comedies eventually had other competitors toward the end of the decade, and only the arrival of the next breakaway hit and changes in the television industry's dynamics really put an end to their run.[44]

Until its last season on the air, *The Beverly Hillbillies* had ratings that put it in the top twenty-five programs. While an affront to notions of high art, *The Beverly Hillbillies* reproduced American values, including ones articulated by the Kennedy administration so ably served by Newton Minow: service to the national family, loyalty, and integrity are more worthy attributes than conspicuous consumption and dishonesty.

[3]

All in the Family

Whereas *The Beverly Hillbillies* went out of its way to avoid controversy, *All in the Family* courted it. In fact, Dorothy Rabinowitz, television critic publishing in *Commentary* in 1975, called *All in the Family*'s creator, Norman Lear, the "entrepreneur of the controversial."[1] That's a fairly accurate label, and Lear may even have liked it. Certainly, he and CBS were quite prepared and, I believe, even hoped for a public eruption when the program aired at midseason, January 1971.

Histories of *All in the Family* suggest that CBS had hesitations about the offensiveness of the program. Indeed, CBS responded in several ways to contain the subject matter of the initial program. Executives encouraged using the milder of two episodes completed as of the air date, and they tussled with Lear about multiple specific moments in the show, eventually achieving concessions on only two matters. Additionally, CBS sent warning notes to its affiliates and requested tolerance while it tried to take new programming directions.[2]

The network alerted the audience by bracketing the program with a disclaimer which declared that the show's function was "ventilating some of the prejudices and misconceptions in American society today." Moreover, the network made both episodes available to the critics for their inaugural reviews, hoping for words of praise.[3]

The premiere episode, "Meet the Bunkers," establishes the generational conflict by contrasting notions about marriage: it revolves around preparations for Archie and Edith's anniversary and uses Archie's early arrival at home, catching Mike and Gloria having sex, to spark debates. The second episode, "Writing the President," exemplifies the soon to be habitual formula of Archie's struggle to best his son-in-law. A debate over watching a TV program on environmental pollution versus watching football highlights of "spooks" (Archie's term for African Americans who he says have inherited genetics for running from animals in the jungle) moves to contrasts between John Wayne and Jack Lemmon, nonnutritional cereals (favored by Archie) and organic food, and good Americans and those protesting race relations and the war. Much of the put-down of Archie exists through his own verbal inadequacies, with malapropisms implying an equivalent inadequacy of thought. Other stereotypes such as Archie's accusation that Catholic nuns spend most of their charity money on golden candlesticks also create this potentially controversial representation.

The histories of the premiere night emphasize that executives such as Robert Wood, in his second year as CBS president, thought the program would be controversial enough to require extra help on the network's telephones. News reports

"I KNOW THAT ARCHIE BUNKER IS REALLY KIDDING, BUT I WONDER IF THE NIGGERS DO."

Sidney Harris for *Broadcasting*

indicate that operators logged only about a thousand calls and 62 percent were tallied as favorable.[4] Overnight Nielsens must have been fairly disappointing when *All in the Family* received only a 15 share.

I write "disappointing" because, for all of the evidence of hesitation and apology, CBS also showed signs of simultaneously hoping to *shock* America. Their description of the new show for *TV Guide* not only "warned" the viewer but tempted as well:

Situation comedy takes a giant step with this adult social satire. This series will explore American prejudices by looking at those of one middle-class family—if viewers can take the heat. There's plenty of abrasive language and subject matter. The family consists of bigoted Archie Bunker (Carroll O'Connor); his spiritless wife Edith (Jean Stapleton); their naively idealistic daughter Gloria (Sally Struthers); and Gloria's husband Mike (Rob Reiner), an argumentative liberal who sorely tries Archie's soul. Mike Evans plays Lionel, a black friend of the younger couple. Tonight, Mike and Archie are wrangling about everything from race to welfare.[5]

Unfortunately, the premiere did not create the explosion that CBS and Lear might have wished. Perhaps part of the cause for that was CBS's choice of leading into *All in the Family* with *Hee Haw* and then pitting it in the New York City area against movies on ABC and NBC (taking 38 and 30 shares). Just not that many people watched the first show.[6]

Moreover, as I shall discuss below, CBS's strategy of turning to the relevant wasn't as original as histories of *All in the Family* sometimes write. And *All in the Family*, as striking as it appeared at the time and retrospectively, was a slow build. Word of mouth and public discussion led viewers to the program, but only over a period of about six months. Ultimately, the public came weekly and somewhat religiously to watch and be shocked, fitting neatly into the plans of CBS. Like *The Beverly Hillbillies, All in the Family* suited well the industrial contexts in which it flourished.

The Initial Contexts and Reception of *All in the Family*

All in the Family came into the CBS lineup in mid-season 1971. However, fall 1970 had already been publicized as the onslaught of "relevancy," with new programs attempting to match recent successes and the temper of the audiences whom advertisers wished to attract. Immediacy, liveness, and visuality had been touted for years as the specialty of television as a medium: film might provide more spectacle and color, but television could bring the living world into the living room. Or even other worlds, as the August 1969 moon landing illustrated. Distances were destroyed while time was the present. For two decades, TV had delivered to American homes remarkable events as they happened: the McCarthy hearings, the on-air shooting of Lee Harvey Oswald, the protests and chaos at the 1968 Democratic convention. What sold TV was relevancy, at least in its news programming. Its entertainment, however, had chosen in the past decade to function as an inexpensive version of movies, with content easily passed by the Motion Picture Association of America. TV family fare was G-rated.

Yet as prime-time TV took over the family entertainment functions that Hollywood had provided for half a century, Hollywood and other media were able to allocate portions of their product to adults. The 1950s and 1960s were decades in which stand-up comedy in clubs and segments of the film business breached more and more taboos. Donna McCrohan finds predecessors to *All in the Family*'s humor in controversial nightclub satirists "such as Lenny Bruce, Mort Sahl, Dick Gregory, Godfrey Cambridge and Jack Burns and Avery Schreiber."[7] Hollywood produced films that tore the Production Code apart by dealing with drug and alcohol addictions, adultery, and homosexuality. Violence and sexual congress had become more and more graphic. In 1968 the Production

Code gave way to the rating system. *Who's Afraid of Virginia Woolf?* (1966) put into the theaters words that usually were confined to saloons (or slips by Dad). *Deep Throat* (1972) was about to be the latest adult must-see. *Easy Rider* (1969) had replaced beach and horror movies as the film for teens, and Hollywood praised as its academy award winners *Patton* (in 1970), *The French Connection* (1971), and *The Godfather* (1972).

Television executives had started the decade of the 1960s with appeals to relevancy and controversy through their news and documentaries. By the middle of the decade, some more edgy entertainment material appeared—always under the protection of contemporary satire and sometimes even disguised as news. *That Was the Week That Was* (NBC) ran for one year in 1964–65, providing immediate and critical commentary on current events. Next up were *The Smothers Brothers Show* (CBS, 1967–69) and *Rowan & Martin's Laugh-In* (NBC, 1968–73).[8] *Laugh-In* garnered blockbuster ratings for its first year, securing an annual average rating of 31.8 in 1968–69 against its nearest competitors, *Gomer Pyle* at 27.2 and *Bonanza* at 26.6. *Laugh-In* still led the ratings in 1969–70 but at a more typical average rating of 26.3.

The cancellation by CBS of *The Smothers Brothers Comedy Hour* has been held up as proof of the conservatism of network executives, and I have no intention of revisiting that series of events here. However, if the traditional stories that executives were trying to control the material are correct, that does not correspondingly imply that the execs were unwilling to seek programs with wide appeal that addressed immediate concerns. The 1970–71 season opened with several new shows marketed as raising socially significant issues, *Marcus Welby* (ABC) being a primary one. Within the drama of medicine, Robert Young transferred his *Father Knows Best* role into current health and education topics. *Marcus Welby* actually won the 1970–71 ratings race, with a yearly average of 29.3, beating out *Flip Wilson* at 27.9 and *Here's Lucy* at 26.1. Other series recognized by critics at the start of the 1970–71 season to be part of the relevancy trend included new drama programs: *The Bold Ones* (NBC), *The Storefront Lawyers* (CBS), and *The Interns* (CBS). New sitcoms considered to have "relevancy" material were *Headmaster* (CBS), *The Mary Tyler Moore Show* (CBS), and *Arnie* (CBS). Even older sitcoms premiered the season with relevancy themes: *The Beverly Hillbillies* and *Lassie* both had pollution issues as drivers to their plots.[9] *Laugh-In* continued to use low-taste, punning, rapid-fire blows; McCrohan writes that the program did an hour of ethnic jokes just weeks before the premiere of *All in the Family*.[10]

On 11 January 1971, *Time*'s cover story was about the amazing box office success of *Love Story* (1970). *Time* interpreted the movie's popularity as an indicator that the "Now Generation and quest for relevance" might be subsiding as President Nixon began to act on promises to withdraw from Vietnam. This forecast proved to be several years off. In hindsight, it is possible to see that debates over social justice and honesty in government would occupy front pages for several more years until the economy weakened in mid-decade, and Nixon, Vietnam, and Watergate were replaced at center stage by a global oil crisis. Black rights, women's liberation, foreign threats in the Middle East and Chile (and U.S. covert attempts to overthrow unwanted governments) would, however, occupy front pages from 1970 until then. In the months of the first episodes of *All in the Family*, the Manson trial concluded in California, Daniel Ellsberg leaked the Pentagon Papers to the media, Nixon announced a trip to China for the following year, the Attica prison riot called attention to violence and racism in U.S. jails, numerous feminist journals including *MS* began publication, and two hundred thousand people marched in protest of the continuing Southeast Asia war in Washington, D.C.

Although I do not believe in easy correlations between viewing behaviors and political and social contexts, it *is* obvious that national debates can command the attention of the public. Playing out these debates in multiple arenas and formulas provides spaces for continuing discussions. The dramatic and melodramatic appeal of argumentation and confrontation among disparate combatants now drives not only drama but news and afternoon talk shows. Violence seems to subtend massive portions of our amusement media. Relevancy, then, had cachet, and sellability to audiences. Moreover, TV had been exploiting relevancy (immediacy and liveness) for several years before the arrival of *All in the Family*. What *All in the Family* did—well, what did *All in the Family* do?

To the critics looking at it during the first three weeks of its airing, it did look like other relevancy programming. As Dwight Newton of the *San Francisco Examiner* detailed, "This 'all-in-the-family' affair wades belly-deep in nearly every challenge confronting nearly every family today—sex, religion, law and order, students, hair, racism, communism—you name it, bumptious Archie Bunker has an opinion."[11]

However, this program *was* different from the others. Some critics found this difference positively innovative; other writers found it offensive, shocking, and tasteless. Those praising it included *Variety,* which wrote:

> This is the best tv comedy since the original "The Honeymooners." It's the best casting since Sgt. Bilko's squad. It should be the biggest hit since "Laugh-in," or the Nielsen sample is in need of severe revision.
>
> . . . Norman Lear and Bud Yorkin have made it as all-American as apple pie, hot dogs, bigotry, ethnic suspicion, political ignorance, social blindness and grandma Moses. . . . Prime element is audacity, generally a benchmark of really imaginative work.[12]

Los Angeles Times reviewer Cecil Smith remarked, "I think it's the happiest and healthiest thing to hit commercial TV since the coaxial cable." Alan Bunce writing for the *Christian Science Monitor* declared that it "marks the first major social departure for this commercial genre [the sitcom]."[13]

Critics found several subordinate features of the program to claim as the characteristics marking its originality. One was its use of farce and satire. As I have suggested, farce and satire were common outside the realm of television, and had appeared on TV in variety format, often through the appearance of guests from stand-up comedy or the music scene (Pete Seeger, Joan Baez). Yet this combination of farce and satire and the sitcom genre seemed a first.

Second, critics favoring the program's innovation often claimed it was real (or some similar term). By "real," however, the critics did not mean it duplicated the routines of everyday life. Rather, they focused on the characters as very recognizable types (often described even by program advocates as stereotypes). Moreover, they considered the intergenerational conflicts as representative of 1970s problems. Realism here wasn't so much a surface familiarity—although the grime and worn furniture of the Bunker household won significant attention as contributing to the effect. *Newsweek* noted, "Despite a family-size package of clichés, 'Family' is the first sitcom ever to present anything even roughly resembling a flesh-and-blood American family."[14] *All in the Family* even won approval from Pamela Haynes, writing for the black publication the *Los Angeles Sentinel*:

The paramount thing about "All in the Family" is that for the first time, instead of trying to pass off an expensively groomed and immaculately coiffed Doris Day as "the typical American housewife" and a distinguished, suave and ever so tolerant Robert [Young] as everyone's father, they have presented a fat, ignorant, angry middle aged pig who swears at his wife, belches at the table and gets choked up over sugary tributes on greeting cards. In other words, Archie Bunker is real.

Far from protesting, members of the minorities slandered by Archie should rejoice at this non-cosmetized portrait of the "master race."[15]

The counter to the endorsement of *All in the Family* was the expectable position that it was tasteless, or even dangerous. While Haynes wrote an appreciative essay for the *Los Angeles Sentinel*, civil rights leader Whitney M. Young, Jr., countered there a week later, arguing that "it has to be a new low in taste." Young went on to suggest: "While the show tries to satirize bigotry, it only succeeds in spreading the poison and making it—by repetition—more respectable." Another critical source was the *New York Times* reviewers. Fred Ferretti believed that the jokes were not humorous, merely poor attempts to shock. Stephanie Harrington took a couple of weeks to consider *All in the Family* and concluded that "'All in the Family' is vulgar and silly. And after the disgust-at-first-shock wears off, the vaudeville clinkers passed off as humor are totally predictable."[16]

This negative evaluation often simply was one of taste: the writer found the program to be in low, or even bad, taste. This view took issue with both the originality and realism claims of the program's proponents. The program might be original, but that didn't justify claims of greatness; the innovation wasn't artful. *Daily Variety* declared: "[T]he idea is valid, but [the] first edition of 'Family,' if this is [an] example of where [the] series is headed, though innovative, is nothing less than an insult to any unbigoted televiewer. . . . [who] is being asked to sit still for a one-joke show—and a sick joke at that." Instead of being realistic, "Archie Bunker plays to the camera as if he were on a vaudeville stage instead of a set that is supposed to be someone's living room. For the home viewer, that little conceit is destroyed anyway by the laughter of the studio audience, which also makes painfully offensive lines that, if not milked for laughs they don't deserve, might at least have some shock value in terms of making people face their prejudices."[17]

Or the negative evaluation could be based on the program's supposed harmful effects. Whitney and others claimed that the satire might not have the effect the producers indicated was their intention—to reduce bigotry. Instead, just the reverse might occur. Bigotry might be made acceptable by the repeated public experience of it without significant repudiation by figures of leadership.

I shall return to this debate about causality; however, during the first two weeks of the program, this issue was already on the table. So, too, were discussions about how humor works. Carroll O'Connor claimed in an interview that comedy was therapeutic.

"A lot of people are going to find it offensive," [O'Connor] said. "They're the people that believe biogtry [*sic*] is like a sore—if you bring it out in the open and scratch it, you'll irritate it and make it worse. They want to hide everything and pretend it doesn't exist.

We believe just the opposite—you bring a thing out in the air and look at it and laugh at it, you'll destroy it.[18]

Norman Lear argued that laughing at ourselves was an American trait.[19]

It didn't take very long for the compromising, transcendent view to be expressed. Maybe the program could both satirize bigotry and also feed into it. Ernie Kreiling writing for the *Valley News* on 5 February 1971 pointed out, "[I]t depends in large measure on the individual." He explained:

There's a basic principle at work in our exposure to the mass media known as selective perception. It simply means we are inclined to read into a message that which is compatible with our existing attitudes, opinions and beliefs. So where "All in the Family" may be designed to parody social illnesses, it may in many instances be reinforcing them among those people who identify with the attitudes being displayed and demonstrated by the Bunker family.[20]

Kreiling's use of social-scientific theory is quite unusual for most newspaper articles. Yet when the communication theorists began to test the claims of effects for *All in the Family*, selective perception theory was one of the first to be considered (see below).

Kreiling did provide one other significant remark: the program was "becoming a national conversation piece." Other papers predicted in their initial reviews that this would happen.[21] The facts are, however, that while consumer surrogates were talking, not very many people were watching. Instead of causing a national furor, the program languished in its time slot with little movement forward in the Nielsen numbers.

In the first reporting period (ending 6 February 1971) after the premiere of *All in the Family*, the program received a Nielsen average rating of 18.1 percent. Its share of the viewing half hour was 21. The estimated number of homes viewing *All in the Family* was 10,880,000; the most-viewed show for that period had 27,050,000 households, although that number was abnormally high for 1971. A more typical most-viewed show in early 1971 ran around 20,000,000. Thus, *All in the Family* secured a viewing audience of only about one-half that of the typical most-viewed program.[22]

Additionally, the Nielsens estimated that of 100 viewing households, *All in the Family* had attracted an average of 65 men (age 18 and up), 80 women, 18 teens (ages 12–17), and 26 children (ages 2–11). In the prime purchasing power category of ages 18–49, *All in the Family* averaged 29 men and 39 women.

When Kreiling's remark that the program was becoming a national conversation item was published in early February, the Nielsen average for *All in the Family* had moved up to only 18.3 percent and a 28 share (for the period ending 20

February 1971). The number of women watching had changed, however, from 80 per 100 viewing households to 91, but men declined from 65 to 60. Teens and children remained basically level at 19 and 24.[23]

The next rating period (ending 1 March 1971) showed a small gain in the average viewing to 18.8 percent; the share moved up to 28. The distribution of viewers, however, returned to 83 women and 66 men. But children (ages 2–11) climbed significantly from the initial figure of 26 to 35. This increase in children and the availability of the program to them would soon become a major part of the debate.[24]

Through February, March, and April 1971, discussion about *All in the Family* continued in the public press. In this second phase of response, the issues previously raised remained in the background while a new, transformed question emerged. The more Archie was watched, the more complex he appeared, and the more "lovable" he became. Can you love a bigot? What are the social effects of loving someone whose beliefs you should abhor?

The attribution of the word "lovable" to Archie occurred early in the reception of *All in the Family*. In fact, "Bill" of *Variety* used the term "lovable bigot" in his initial review, and others applied the adjective as well.[25] At least two reasons might exist for this initial declaration. One is that the series' publicity and interviews primed the pump. More important, though, is the immediate association reviewers made with an earlier, milder version of Archie. From the start, critics compared *All in the Family* to *The Honeymooners*, and Archie to Ralph Kramden as played by Jackie Gleason.[26] While Archie was seen as novel, he was also perceived as within a heritage of the bumbling, working-class,[27] white, male husband, a staple of early 1950s television that had only in the 1960s been superseded by the superdad.[28]

Thus, the sitcom context set up reviewers to like Archie. Moreover, even some critics who were initially put off by Archie's language and views found themselves, nearly against their wills, being drawn into his conceptual universe. Writing for the *Saturday Review*, Robert Lewis Shayon warned, "Each week, Archie is involved harmlessly in a situation that permits him to verbalize freely an abundance of in-group hostilities. . . . Archie wins, Archie loses, but his ethnocentrism is never breached. He awaits next week's lovable encounter with Catholics, Jews, blacks, hippies, commies, et al., with unredeemed lovable hatred."[29]

On the reverse side, one writer who seemed to have initially disliked the program was now being drawn into it, but for the opposite reason. Norman Mark for the *Chicago Daily News* confessed, "I've watched *All in the Family* several times now since its premiere last month, and I'm beginning to change my mind once more about this important new series. . . . It is on the cutting edge of TV innovation, and it is slowly unveiling more complexities within its characters." Mark noted an important part in his shifting view was that Archie seemed to be winning some of the arguments, and Mark implied that some of Archie's views *were* worth listening to.[30]

Other writers disagreed that Archie was occasionally articulating the successful point. Jack Gould for the *New York Times* suggested, "It is easy to misunderstand 'All in the Family,' to concentrate on Archie's disparagement of practically everyone around him. The larger lesson is that he is continually a loser, always a bit more frustrated than before." John Leonard for *Life* lambasted the series for two "lies." One was that Archie represented working men. The other was that "Mr. O'Connor's Archie is, anyway, charming. Forgivable."[31]

Unable to conclude in isolated argumentation whether Archie was or was not, should or should not be made complex or lovable, and was or was not winning any arguments, surrogate consumers referred to those people whom Archie was demeaning to settle the debates. And they referred to all sorts of other experts that might give or withhold approval. Gould mentioned that "some sensitive community groups involving blacks, whites and the clergy" had given the program "sympathetic approval." Lear used the opportunity of an interview to provide all sorts of evidence that the program was acceptable: the Nielsens were up, mail was twenty to thirty to one in favor of the program, sociology classes were using the show, and people were asking for scripts. (Read: "the people" and teachers thought it was okay.) *Newsweek* mentioned that "critic Cleveland Amory of *TV Guide* calls it simply 'the best show on television.'" (A major surrogate consumer had made his decision.) Moreover, black press reviews praised it and critics were relooking at it now that the shock was over. (If blacks and critics liked it . . . !) Shayon in *Saturday Review* repeated the stories Lear gave about the 70–80 percent favorable mail and requests for study guides for the program, and he added that people who normally didn't watch TV were.[32]

This period of a "snowballing" in support for *All in the Family* (with reviewers actually picking up commentary, arguments, and evidence from other writers) was not without dissent, and even within some of the essays which were generally positive about the series, negative comments occurred. However, in general in the spring of 1971, more and more attention was being paid to the mixed response to Archie's character and its possible negative effects. Meanwhile, the Nielsens only crept upward. For the rating period ending 17 April, *All in the Family*'s average rating was 17.9 percent; the share had increased to 27. The question now was, should the program be renewed for the next season? The answer to that was within the hands of Wood and other CBS executives.[33]

Out with the Old and In with the "Best Show"

Although Amory of *TV Guide* had pronounced that *All in the Family* was "not just the best-written, best-directed and best-acted show on television, it is the best show on television,"[34] network executives were not about to renew a program that could not bring in advertising dollars. It was not the case that *All in the Family* was a sure bet for renewal when CBS made its famous sweeping cancellation of longtime network leaders. Instead, the story of maintaining *All in the Family* in the lineup is a bit more complex. The traditional story is that CBS shifted from programming appealing to older, rural audience members to shows that had better demographics for advertising income. While that was certainly the plan, what kind of programs would attract the "right" audience was not obvious at immediate glance.[35]

As mentioned earlier, CBS president Wood was already on record at the start of the 1970–71 season as in the process of updating CBS's network image. In fact, while the shake-up likely was in the planning by October 1969, Wood officially announced the strategy at the May 1970 CBS affiliates' meeting, advertising a "young, fresh, new approach to programming."[36] In the next month, he promoted Fred Silverman to head programmer for CBS.

Wood and CBS's decision derives in large part from late 1960s information about TV audiences. As far back as January 1967, a Harris poll suggested that television was "losing its appeal for better-educated, more affluent viewers," and in April of that year, a Television Information Office survey indicated that while TV was the major news source for 64 percent of adults, "positive opinions of entertainment programming have noticeably declined in the past year."[37]

These were obviously discouraging bits of information, and scarcely news that TV executives wanted their advertisers to hear. For the season of 1968–69, NBC took at least two innovative steps: it premiered *Laugh-In*, which became the top season rating getter, and it programmed *Julia*. Starring Diahann Carroll, *Julia* was widely discussed since it was novel in presenting a middle-class African American female as the show's central character, and, more important, the program was a rating success, coming in seventh for the season with an average rating of 24.6 percent. At NBC, Paul Klein had initially promoted *Julia* as a "public good" show, assuming almost any show NBC put opposite CBS's *Red Skelton* would lose the time slot. Its surprise triumph also suggested that instead of targeting everyone, programming might address specific audiences—a lesson Hollywood had also only recently discovered (although also facilitated by changes in advertising practices).[38]

Newly appointed CBS president Wood not only noted that NBC aimed its programming at youth but, worse, that although CBS led the three networks, the programs supporting that position were attended to by mostly older viewers, obviously becoming even older. These were definitely not the people advertisers wished to seek. Advertisers would rather have fewer people but the ones more likely to purchase the goods or services being promoted. Moreover, as Les Brown recounts in his history of the period, Wood not only wanted to change these demographic dynamics but to wrest control from CBS programmer Michael Dann.[39] For the 1970–71 season, CBS dropped *Red Skelton* and also *Jackie Gleason, Petticoat Junction,* and *Gomer Pyle, USMC.* Remaining in the lineup were other rural comedies including *Andy Griffith/Mayberry RFD, The Beverly Hillbillies,* and *Green Acres.* Still pulling strong numbers, these shows also filled up the CBS prime time while replacements could be developed.

Anecdotes about the discovery of *All in the Family* habitually describe the failure of ABC to pick up two earlier pilot episodes floated by Lear and Bud Yorkin in early 1969. A revised pilot with the eventual cast of *All in the Family* reached the screening room of new CBS head of programming Silverman during the summer of 1970. Silverman had worked at CBS from 1963 under Dann. Writing a master's thesis about ABC's programming practices, Silverman coined the phrase the "get-age" families to refer to people in the age brackets most likely to be major purchasers and, of course, those to be treasured by advertisers. Silverman's thesis promoted other programming strategies including counterprogramming, linking shows that might have a flow in audiences, and "crossplugging" in which a star in one program appears in another show. Most of all, his thesis encouraged seeking a youth audience. From all accounts, Silverman was enthused by the pilot for *All in the Family*, and Wood readily concurred. *All in the Family* went into production during the fall for premiering in January 1971.[40]

During the spring of 1971 the questions of renewal not only of *All in the Family* but of other longtime workhorses for CBS was in question. Yet ratings for the old favorites declined while *All in the Family*'s were on an upswing. *Mayberry RFD* was in the process of dropping from fourth-highest rated program to fifteenth (for 1970–71) with an annual average rating moving from 24.4 to 22.3. *The Beverly Hillbillies*, ranked eighteenth in 1969–70, could not reach the top twenty-five for 1970–71. *Green Acres* had failed to make that plateau for both 1969–70 and 1970–71. During the week of 22 March 1971, CBS canceled twelve programs, including all of the above and *The Ed Sullivan Show*.[41]

The cancellation of those shows, while boding well for *All in the Family*, did not ensure its renewal. In late March, *All in the Family* was still struggling. For the period ending 3 April the program's rating was one of its lowest to date at 17.1 percent and its share was only 26. However, on 14 April, the National Academy of Television Arts and Sciences announced its Emmy nominations. Included in the "outstanding comedy series" and several other award categories was CBS's *All in the Family* as well as CBS's also-new *The Mary Tyler Moore Show*. On 21 April, CBS signed up both of the series for the next season.[42]

Beyond the visibility and potential publicity provided by the Emmy nominations, *All in the Family* had several other competitive advantages even if its ratings were still languishing. These related to shifting industrial factors. For one thing, *All in the Family*'s verbal shock might substitute for visual violence as a means of attracting viewers. The networks were particularly sensitive to accusations that excessive violence flooded prime time. In the summer of 1968 the National Commission on the Causes and Prevention of Violence began its hearings. In December 1968, it reported that TV was a "'corrosive force'" in this matter, echoing complaints against television raised in the 1961 congressional hearings on juvenile delinquency and TV violence which targeted programs such as *The Untouchables* (off the air since 1963). ABC president Leonard H. Goldenson and CBS president Frank Stanton promised (again) that they were taking steps to respond. In 1970 the Department of Health, Education, and Welfare funded twenty-three projects on the effects of television on children.[43]

All in the Family might offer stimulation other than violence. Moreover, its shock value might also increase retention of related advertising, *and* it might pull in youth viewers—the baby boomers once watching *The Beverly Hillbillies*. Financially, these two considerations had high priority for all of the networks. Part of this interest in improving and securing successful advertising dynamics derived from the loss of cigarette money in January 1971 when the networks agreed to ban that industry's product from the commercial airwaves. Cable also finally appeared as a competitor, potentially weakening the oligopoly held by the three major firms. The loss of revenue (15 percent for January 1971 and 9 percent for February 1971) produced creative strategies to shore up income. In

March 1971 CBS decided to split its commercial time lengths from sixty seconds to thirty seconds, ending up with more revenue for two ads than for the previous one. ABC and NBC followed suit.[44]

However, selling more advertising spots (at a financial gain) required strong evidence that advertisers were obtaining what they paid for. Evidence of the past decade provided no clear answers. In 1962 a Young and Rubicam study suggested that "no evidence [existed] that program content influences the effectiveness of commercials," but the Schwerin Research Corporation rapidly countered that its findings concluded that "program mood does affect the viewing public's retention of commercial messages." During the summer of 1971, Harvard research concluded that preschoolers could not distinguish ads from programs but teens were "critical of commercials to the point of cynicism."[45] None of these studies provided support that would indicate a program that was controversial would improve ad retention, but shock might still serve as a useful means of differentiating the experience from the rest of TV's flow.

For a third point, *All in the Family* did not have great ratings in mid-April, but the demographic groups in which its ratings were increasing were the right ones. Although data are not available from these categories for the two-week period ending 8 May, the statistics are accessible for the one ending 22 May. While these figures are somewhat skewed because they follow the rush to watch the program after it won four Emmys, the general trend can still be inferred. From the ratings period ending 6 February to the one ending 22 May, the number of men watching *All in the Family* per 100 viewing households changed from 65 to 68. However, the number of women went from 80 to 92, and this is in a climate in which women were generally preferred viewers because of their lead in household purchasing habits.[46] Teens moved from 18 to 20, and children slightly dropped from 26 to 24. Eventually, however, when *All in the Family* moved at the start of the fall 1971 season from Tuesday evenings at 9:30 P.M. to Saturdays at 8:00 P.M., the number of children rose dramatically to 37. The number even moved up into the 30s during the summer (when school wasn't a hindrance to later evening viewing).[47]

Not only was the program pulling strong demographics among women (and eventually children), but the women watching were in the right age bracket. The figures show 58 women in the prime purchasing ages of 18 to 49. Moreover, the 50-plus women bracket was declining (from an initial 41 to 34), as was the 50-plus men (36 to 25). The pickup in the men echoed the women: 29 to 43 in the 18-to-49 age category. Although I am anticipating the story a bit, by the end of 1971, Yorkin was asserting that *All in the Family* was pulling a 70 share for New York City. In a study published in 1976, Timothy P. Meyer writes that Nielsens showed that *All in the Family* drew in people across all ages, education, and socioeconomic levels, and it also had "the largest child audience for any regular TV show."[48]

Thus, for CBS the renewal of *All in the Family* based on its Emmy nominations was a smart move in hopes that peer recognition would validate the program for audiences. More significantly, though, the ratings were improving and in just the right categories. Since demographics drove corporate decision making throughout the history of broadcasting in the United States, renewal became a fairly easy call.

When *All in the Family* actually won three of the most prestigious Emmy categories three weeks later on 12 May, CBS took out major ads in prime locations including *Variety.* The ads ran through a gamut of adjectives that were culled from critical responses: "freshness," "courage," "breakthrough," and "landmark."[49] This publicity had at least two goals. One was to mark the program as different from anything else in the recent past and most certainly on contemporary television. Another was to emphasize the new look for CBS. No longer the sedate network, it was into the running for the baby boomer generation's attention. In the rating period following the Emmy broadcast, *All in the Family* won second place among all shows, beaten out only by the Emmy broadcast itself. Moreover, in the seventy major-market cities, it was number one.[50] For CBS in May 1971, the future of *All in the Family* looked promising, and it turned out just that way. But some of the major discussions over the program were just about to occur.

The Hobson Incident

During the first six months of *All in the Family* not only were taboo words, actions, and sounds (e.g., toilet flushings) represented, but the program ventured into numerous subject areas previously avoided on television. *All in the Family* tackled racism (was Archie now part black, having received blood from a black donor?) and stereotypes (Archie insisted that

Jewish lawyers represent him in a lawsuit; Archie misjudged who was and was not a homosexual). Very personal family matters were considered: Archie tried to help Mike who seemed to be having an impotency problem; Gloria experienced a miscarriage. None of these situations was uncommon or undiscussed in films or newspapers and magazines at the time. The novelty was their uncontrolled appearance on prime time and entrance into homes and into the minds of young viewers.

The fall 1971 season solidified *All in the Family* as the number one television program in the nation (and shortly elevated it to the status of a blockbuster hit), but it also witnessed continuing concerns about effects, with influence on children developing into a major issue. This concern occurred in part because CBS moved *All in the Family* to Saturday nights at 8 P.M. as a lead-in to its lineup of relevancy comedies, with the other Emmy award winner, *The Mary Tyler Moore Show,* bookending the two-hour flow at 9:30 P.M.[51] In a very smart move, instead of relegating Saturday evening to mediocre programming, Silverman and Wood elevated it to an adult TV night—or at least a night for which dates started later than they might have previously. Moreover, children as well as adults now had access to the program.

This increased accessibility was a partial motivator for Laura Z. Hobson to write her essay "As I Listened to Archie Say 'Hebe' . . . ," but its appearance in the 12 September 1971 *New York Times* likely had the reverse effect from the one she may have wished. For her essay rejuvenated the discussions about the possible impacts of *All in the Family.* These discussions refocused public attention on the program, bringing in viewers who would judge for themselves whether or not the program was good or bad for the nation. By the end of the fall, *All in the Family* was capturing a 70 share for New York City and routinely securing ratings in the mid-30s. For the period ending 18 December 1971, *All in the Family* had a 35.2 percent rating and a 57 share for the nation. Moreover its numbers for the right categories of viewers were stronger than in late spring. Men were at 74 per 100 viewing households; women at 95. Teens continued at 20, but children had risen dramatically to 41 (from an initial 26). Men in the 18–49 age bracket numbered 42; women in the 18–49 category were 53. While no stronger than in May, these 18–49 figures did suggest that the move to Saturday night had not adversely impacted numbers for the prime adult audiences.[52]

Hobson had specific credentials to criticize *All in the Family*. She was author of *Gentlemen's Agreement*, a novel which in the postwar United States stood out as a major attack on bigotry. In her 12 September article, Hobson reviewed the praise and disgust expressed by various writers, but then she moved to a more particular and new charge: it was not just that the program could not be an effective tool against bigotry because Archie was too lovable and the program wasn't tough enough on racism, but that it avoided the really taboo terms: "nigger," "kike," and so forth. She continued,

And one thing that's nearly as nasty as exposing these millions, and their children, week after week to bigotry, is to expose them constantly to hypocrisy.

Particularly since more children than ever will be watching in the new season. . . .[53]

Hobson's charge about the cushioning effects of repeatedly ex-periencing bigotry had been a major theme in the spring. Her accusations of hypocrisy and child endangerment were new.

Rapidly, Lear responded. As a Jewish person he had cer-tainly reacted to the words used in the program: "yid," "Hebe," and even "Jew." Lear defended Archie as a different case from some bigots. Archie was motivated by fear not by hate, which was why Archie could be characterized as so com-plex and, yes, "lovable." Then Lear proposed that Hobson herself might also be prejudiced. In her list of unused terms, she did not include "schwartze." Lear pondered why, hy-pothesizing, "She didn't object because she doesn't associate the highly educated, very sophisticated, upper-class individual who uses the word schwartze with a common, lower-class bigot like Archie Bunker."[54]

Hobson's essay set off a new round of debates. Many of the same themes from the spring returned. Rejoinders were simi-lar. Writers marshaled evidence of praise and rebuke from various minority organizations, including the fact that when Sammy Davis, Jr., indicated he very much wanted to appear on the show, the writers created a part for him in which he kissed Archie on-screen.[55] However, two events in this cycle are worthy of notice: responses by Arnold Hano and the aca-demic community.

In March 1972, Hano provided a lengthy article to the *New York Times Magazine* entitled "Can Archie Bunker Give Bigotry a Bad Name?" As in his essay in November 1963 in which he summarized the discussions over *The Bev-erly Hillbillies* and the "G.A.P"—the great American pub-lic—Hano articulated an argument for the popular and against the cultural elite. Referring to the head of the Anti-Defamation League of the B'nai B'rith, the late Whitney Young, Jr., of the Urban League, and Hobson, he labeled them "ethnic professionals." It was not obvious that they represented the mass: "Once again we are witnessing a dichotomy between the so-called intellectual leaders of the community and the rest of us poor slobs."[56] Abstaining from using the ratings to make his claim, he reconstructed the question to be, "Is this a show that is bad for America?" His answer: the program proved that Americans were not interested in trivia or escapism and that they could laugh at themselves. Such a conclusion boded well for the country.

A bit sarcastic, Hano's label of the "ethnic professional" did direct attention to the irony that, as with the case of *The Beverly Hillbillies*, much of the commentary came from two sets of liberals at odds regarding the production of culture. As writers for the *Nation* pointed out in November 1971, "Much of the criticism [of *All in the Family*] has tended to fester, not in *TV Guide* or among the intellectually unanointed but in middling highbrow and liberal circles."[57] Of course, Lear, Carroll O'Connor, and many other advocates of the program also considered themselves liberal and highbrow.

What both groups had in common was a desire to use the medium of television for education. Both groups likely supported public broadcasting and *Masterpiece Theatre*. Both groups likely were democrats, and interested in the growing Watergate scandal as an opportunity to unmask "Tricky Dicky."[58] What split the groups apart were theories of media, communication, and culture.

With a national debate of this magnitude ongoing, scholars

leaped into the field to resolve the issues. One of the earliest attempts was the work of John Slawson in *Educational Broadcasting Review* in April 1972, just a bit over one year after the premiere of the program. Slawson's essay was a think piece. He had not accomplished any research specifically on *All in the Family*, but he used other work to make inferences. For example, he brought up the findings of the 1969 Commission on the Causes and Prevention of Violence that concluded that "exposure [to representations of violence] tends to *stimulate* violent behavior, rather than divert aggressive impulses to harmless channels." He also suggested a "halo effect" might occur.[59]

The first effects studies began to appear in 1974. Given that contemporary national concern over the effects of violence had focused particularly on children, effects studies of *All in the Family* usually sought to distinguish results by ages and educational levels. As mentioned earlier, one of the first reports used the selective perception hypothesis to construct its research, and crossed that with the selective exposure hypothesis (the assumption that people will watch a program less if it does not conform to their values and beliefs). Results of that study and others produced conclusions which were shortly rejected by other studies or which were so limited in scope as to have questionable wider significance.[60]

Social scientists did not uniformly believe the program might have a proclivity to reinforce prejudices; however, the majority were inclined toward that conclusion. Humanist scholars tended to analyze the narrative dynamics of the program as illustrative of American culture or to cite its innovative textual construction within a somewhat turgid TV flow.[61]

Whatever were the actual effects of *All in the Family* on individuals, culturally and industrially the program was significant. Issues widely current in public discussion received even more exposure, turning up in the one place somewhat sacrosanct to this point: prime-time entertainment television. Often used as a signifier of the program's meaning, the installation of the Bunker living room in the Smithsonian Institution in September 1978 sealed its place in American history.

Moreover, the program participated in a major transition in television programming. Its rating and share success—initially through attracting the right demographics—also implied that target marketing had credibility. No one expected another breakaway of the magnitude of *All in the Family*, but a good living could result from careful appeals to specific segments of the American public. *All in the Family* ended its second season (1971–72) with an average rating of 34.0, 5.8 percentage points ahead of number two *Flip Wilson*. It remained a breakaway leader for 1972–73 (33.3 percent, 5.7 ahead of *Sanford & Son*) and 1973–74 (31.2, 3.2 over *The Waltons*). (One might also note that race issues were available for reading in *Flip Wilson* and *Sanford & Son* as well.) The show held onto the leadership through the seasons of 1974–75 and 1975–76; its run of five years in first place is matched only by *The Cosby Show*. Another tribute to its achievement is the number of spin-offs and imitators that rapidly appeared in the wake of its achievement: *Sanford & Son, Good Times, The Jeffersons, Chico and the Man, Maude. All in the Family* may not have been the first television program to take advantage of the relevancy trend and shock strategies, but it was exceptionally successful and influential. In that sense, it continued the drive of network broadcasting to take advantage of television's opportunity to offer consumers immediacy, liveness, and visuality. And to sell those consumers to advertisers.

[4]

Laverne & Shirley

In fall 1975, a New York City exhibitor tried to explain the phenomenon of the midnight movie. His explanation was that the youth of ages eighteen to twenty-five had "nothing to do. Nothing. Zero!" Of these nothings, the choices seemed to be two: "[E]very kid who owns a pair of blue jeans thinks he's gonna find the spirit of his generation in a midnight movie house. Forget it; it's all crummy kink, banal camp, bad sex."[1] The other choice, as one potential moviegoer disenchanted with crummy kink, banal camp, and bad sex proposed, was to go home and see what was on the tube.

What was on the tube in fall 1975 for one of the prime markets of television advertisers? The top-rated show from the previous season had been *All in the Family,* which was returning to begin its fifth season and still plying its relevancy appeals. However, down in the pack was *Happy Days,* having premiered the season before, but starting the fall 1975 season with "a new theme song . . . plus an apparent new focus on Fonzie the dropout."[2] *Happy Days* had been initially described by *Variety* as "another dose of the escapist razzmatazz that nostalgic lookbacks should only remember the simple pleasures (and stereotypes) of a past era."[3] But the fore-grounding of Fonzie and the success of an episode involving two working-class girls which produced the spin-off *Laverne & Shirley* starting in January 1976 would alter the TV scene. When *Laverne & Shirley* premiered in mid-season, it took top ratings for the week. *Variety* indicated that the program's debut rating at 35.1 was the highest debut numbers in ten years. By the end of the ratings week of 11 April 1976, *Laverne & Shirley* had tied with *All in the Family* for top average ratings of the second season, and for the 1975–76 season ranked third at 27.2 against *All in the Family*'s 30.1.[4] During the next year, *Happy Days* and *Laverne & Shirley* became ratings busters—top-rated programs that significantly outran their second- or third-ranked competitors. In this case, *Happy Days* and *Laverne & Shirley* averaged 31.5 and 30.9 respectively for the year, significantly ahead of the third-ranked program, *ABC Monday Night Movies*, which came in at a season's average of only 26. The same blockbuster phenomenon occurred for the 1977–78 season, with *Laverne & Shirley* outdoing *Happy Days* 31.6 to 31.4, and the third-rated program, *Three's Company*, over 3 points behind at 28.3.

Like its parent program, *Laverne & Shirley* was set two decades previously, in the 1950s, and, like its parent, critics initially described *Laverne & Shirley* as evoking nostalgia for the simplicity of that generation. Thus, if young adults did turn on the tube, they could find some relevancy comedy, but their primary TV choice was a spectacle quite unlike what they would see in the movie houses of most midsized

American cities. In fact, their TV choice was much like their option in moviegoing: the relevant and iconoclastic *The Rocky Horror Picture Show*, which appealed to a small, urban young adult audience, versus the broad-based escapist heroics of *Jaws* (1975), *Rocky* (1976), and *Star Wars* (1977), all blockbuster movies fueled by youth attendance. Thus, the two dominant entertainment options for the 18-to-25 crowd in both media had similar ranges of diversity, with TV's options still constrained by its family setting and small image.

The apparent utopian desire for a more innocent, simpler, and nobler time, however, is only part of the cause for the achievements of *Laverne & Shirley*. Other factors include specific changes in the broadcasting industry and ABC's programming practices, and, very important, textual factors of *Laverne & Shirley*. Thus, I must emphasize that while *Happy Days* set the ratings stage for *Laverne & Shirley*, *Laverne & Shirley* altered the play, bringing new factors into the mid-1970s TV flow. It is *Laverne & Shirley* that pulled *Happy Days* up to its number one ratings, producing the dyad that would lead other programming in the late 1970s. Understanding these events requires discussing both programs as contributing to the TV blockbuster event.

The Initial Reception of *Happy Days*

Happy Days' appeal to young adults was on the basis of "nostalgia." The program hoped to share in the reception of recent movie hits such as *American Graffiti* (1973). Creators Tom Miller, Edward Milkis, and Garry Marshall began developing

Happy Days in early 1970 (before *All in the Family*'s arrival) and specifically at the suggestion of Michael Eisner, then an ABC programming executive. *Happy Days'* appeal was to be similar to that of *I Remember Mama*, a look back at the time when the young couples who would be the prospective audience were growing up. Rather than being a 1950s program set in the 1930s, *Happy Days* would reproduce the 1970s young-adult generation's adolescence in the 1950s. Yet Eisner rejected verbal pitches by Miller and Milkis on the grounds the franchise would be "too soft."

In 1972 Marshall managed to finance a pilot by doing a segment for *Love, American Style* (an anthology series), starring Ron Howard, Anson Williams, Marion Ross, and Harold Gould. (Eventually the first three would go on to take up their roles in the series.) The segment had enough interest that Eisner supported continued development, and Miller and Milkis convinced Eisner to give series approval in 1973 when they could also plan to use adjacent publicity that Howard was gathering from starring in the "companion" film, *American Graffiti*.[5]

Thus, when *Happy Days* premiered in January 1974 critics immediately connected it to and compared it with *American Graffiti* under the common umbrella of "nostalgia."[6] The dictionary defines *nostalgia* as "homesickness" and "a longing for things, persons, or situations that are not present." However, what home has been lost, what things, persons, or situations are missed, or imagined to be missing, can be quite different, and, indeed, the nostalgia created by *American Graffiti* is quite different from the one first attempted and then eventually evoked by *Happy Days*.[7]

Thus, to explain the reception of *Happy Days* and later *Laverne & Shirley*, it is important to review briefly what surrogate consumers thought of *American Graffiti,* because that film's reception influenced the initial expectations for *Happy Days.* When critics were unhappy that the program didn't turn out like the film, its creators readjusted the formula in ways that would set the stage for a further alteration in *Laverne & Shirley.* This is a case of tinkering with elements until structures work for the audiences that will watch the formula.

The critics' comparison of *Happy Days* to *American Graffiti* certainly had merit. Both *Happy Days* and *American Graffiti* purported to represent nearly the same time period and nearly the same set of people—high schoolers and their rituals prior to the assassination of John F. Kennedy, the sexual revolution, the civil rights movement, and the Vietnam War. Moreover, Howard starred in both the film and the TV series, and Cindy Williams, also in *American Graffiti,* would play Shirley in *Laverne & Shirley.* What was noticeably different were the types of homes the characters came from in *American Graffiti* and *Happy Days.* A great deal of the variance had to do with textual differences. Some of it was attributable to the ultimate generic differences between the male-centered melodrama of *American Graffiti* and the situation comedy of *Happy Days*; some of it was also due to different ideas of what had intervened between the 1950s and the 1970s that would cause one to long for the 1950s. But whatever the causes, the differences are illuminating for explaining the reactions of surrogate consumers when they first viewed *Happy Days.*

American Graffiti was specifically labeled as a "nostalgic" film by five of the seven reviewers I surveyed.[8] Moreover, the language they used is consistent in suggesting that what was lost was the innocence of youth and the security of small-town life, both left behind. If the reviewer attributed a cause to these losses of innocence and security, he or she referred to a subsequent recognition that the 1950s were actually quite superficial compared with the present day and that the domestic and international violence of the 1960s had altered global consciousness. Here are some examples:

1. [The film's] milieu is the accumulated junk and materialism of the Eisenhower years, an endowment of tin theology and synthetic values which, in younger generations, sowed the seeds of an incoherent unrest that would mature violently a decade later.[9]

2. Set at the tail end of an era, the film freezes the last moment of American innocence. In 1962 the kids in Modesto still drive fifties cars, listen to fifties music, and pattern themselves after fifties culture heroes—James Dean, Connie Stevens, Sandra Dee. It's as if they were trying to make time stand still. They can't know how radically the country will be shaken and polarized by the cataclysms of the next few years; but they do have an intuitive sense that their culture is disintegrating. . . . the comedy is displaced by a growing sense of wistfulness and melancholy. . . . [the film] recalls the innocence and the sense of community—the shared language, music and humor that contributed to the last authentic national folk culture. . . . For those of us in Lucas's generation, watching *American Graffiti* is like going home; it's a primal experience, and the deeply conflicting feelings that it stirs cannot possibly be resolved.[10]

3. What makes *American Graffiti* so extraordinary a film is not that it recreates for us the world's innocence but that it recreates our own innocence. It evokes an unreachable time.[11]

Doubtless, these reactions of melancholy were provoked in major part by the ending of the film, in which two of the characters' futures involve the Vietnam War: one is missing in action; another is a writer in Canada.

Contrast that nostalgia to the nostalgia evoked by *Happy Days*. The emphasis was still on the innocence of the 1950s, but that innocence was couched not in the arena of the political or public sphere but rather in private terms—more specifically, it was sexual innocence. What critics of *Happy Days* perceived was that the series was *not* discussing the intervention in Vietnam, the antiwar crisis, or any enfeeblement as a nation, but rather the sexual liberation movement—an oddly antithetical event to these others. What the United States lost in national power, its populace gained in personal power, but at the cost of sexual reserve.

Such a shift in narrative dynamics might be accounted for by the shift from film to television and perhaps justified by the shift in nostalgic tone from the melancholic to the comic. However, in comparison with *American Graffiti*, the critics, not surprisingly, found *Happy Days* wanting: "References to Eisenhower, Milton Berle, 'I, the Jury' and hairdos do not 1950s nostalgia make any more than the excesses of a laugh track create comedy." "'Happy Days' is another dose of the escapist razzmatazz that nostalgic lookbacks should only remember the simple pleasures (and stereotypes) of a past era"; it is a "pseudonostalgia." Powerful critic Cleveland Amory of *TV Guide* called it a "nostalgic comedy" and "awful."[12] Thus, in relation to its apparent source, *Happy Days* was found seriously wanting.

In January 1974, *All in the Family* continued to top the

ratings. Although some liberal critics remained concerned about the possible interpretations of the program by racists and children, *All in the Family* seemed a paragon of social relevance in comparison with the personal conservatism offered by *Happy Days*. Television may not have yet wandered out of the vast wasteland, but *All in the Family* was closer to intellectual civilization than this new series. Nothing in the surrogate consumers' commentary recommended *Happy Days* to its viewers.

Critics were not, however, unmindful of the problem that the American populace was sometimes not as prepared as they were to take on serious issues in prime time. They did speculate about what might make the program work: "Bok" for *Variety* suggested that Howard's "long-time appeal as a kid actor, dating back to the 'Andy Griffith Show,' and his current presence in 'American Graffiti'" might pull in audiences.[13] Indeed, a goodly number of people tuned in to the first episodes of *Happy Days*, perhaps to see how Little Opie was doing. Initial ratings of *Happy Days* placed it twenty-second in the rankings for the Nielsen period ending 9 February 1974, but in the next few weeks it failed to reach the top twenty-five list. Viewers of the first episodes were fairly well distributed in terms of demographics. In 100 viewing households, 62 viewers were men (46 in the 18 to 49 age category), 71 were women (54 ages 18 to 49), 31 teens, and 57 children. Compare this with *All in the Family* in December 1971 when it had reached number one status: 74 men (42 ages 18 to 49); 95 women (53 ages 18 to 49), 20 teens and 41 children. Thus, *Happy Days* had good distribution and even exceeded *All in the Family* among teens and children (considered valuable audiences) but was behind numerically. Moreover, in subsequent weeks, viewership of men dropped off. Ratings languished around the average of 21.0.[14]

What kept *Happy Days* on television was the fact that programming executives look at a show in relation to the entire schedule. Here industry practices intervened. For one thing, despite an overall less than spectacular showing, *Happy Days* was doing well in the time period of Tuesday 8 P.M. It was taking a 33 share, and doing that against *Maude*, in *Maude*'s first season as a spin-off of *All in the Family*.[15]

This was not only a specific battle between shows but, more significantly, an act of aggression by a weaker network, ABC, against longtime powerhouse CBS. This competition was not merely symbolic, of course, but directly influential in terms of revenues. For years, industry personnel concentrated on which networks were weekly and nightly winners. *Variety* articles habitually calculate who "wins" each night. The reason for this lies in the theory of flow of audiences. If a strong show with the right demographics can pull in an audience early in the evening, the audiences are likely to remain with the network through the evening, into the news, and then the late night show. The channel left on when going to bed is the one there when the TV is turned on the next morning. Winning nights thus means that a network is generally controlling a good portion of the audience, and advertising rates can be levied accordingly. Taking Tuesday night would be financially very beneficial for ABC.

For a second thing, *Happy Days* was the third highest rated show among women ages 18 to 49, "generally considered television's most lucrative audience," as the *Wall Street Jour-*

nal explained it in March 1974. And, for a third thing, research and press reports indicated that *Happy Days* "was a rare show for TV—one that seemed to grasp every demographic."[16] Thus, the program's audience mix looked promising, and permitting it to build might pay off in the long run. In the hand of cards that ABC held, *Happy Days* seemed relatively stronger than many other programs.

No doubt nostalgia for simpler times was appealing to some of its audience, and its escapism came as a relief from so much else that was happening on television in the spring of 1974. Only as recently as October 1973, Spiro Agnew had resigned as vice-president, and Watergate was ongoing with impeachment hearings to start in July 1974, culminating in Nixon's resignation in August. Additionally, what families were was significantly changing. PBS's documentary *An American Family*, chronicling the Louds of Santa Barbara, California, had run during 1973; unexpected at the start of the filming was the eventual disintegration of the family unit with Bill and Pat Loud divorcing. This representation of American life was not atypical. As Donna McCrohan suggests in *Prime Time, Our Time*, a crisis over the "traditional family" may have accounted for part of the escapist appeal of *Happy Days*. McCrohan notes that "by 1978, only one family in four fit the traditional dad-works-mom-cooks pattern, and couples with no children under 18 represented 47 percent of all families." As many as 40 percent of children born in the 1970s were in single-parent homes.[17]

Gender relations were in flux. Feminism and women's liberation were dominant social themes. In September 1973 Billie Jean King had beaten Bobby Riggs in a highly publicized battle-of-the-sexes tennis match. Finally, around 1973 and deepening in the next couple of years was a major recession as a consequence of the oil crisis. Unemployment and prices rose. Looking to the past—one remembered by young married couples or imagined by children—must certainly have had attraction. Even if the nostalgia was not of the sort offered by *American Graffiti* and praised by surrogate consumers, American television viewers apparently enjoyed the comedy offered in *Happy Days*.[18] This enticement was enough to continue the program on the air, but it was insufficient to take *Happy Days* to any remarkable stage in the ratings race and the consciousness of the American public.

Reworking *Happy Days* and the Arrival of *Laverne & Shirley*

For one and one-half years, *Happy Days* maintained its rating status. NBC had moved *Maude* in the fall of 1974; *Happy Days* continued to function as a good lead into ABC's Tuesday night lineup. At the end of the 1974–75 season, *Happy Days* had average spring 1975 ratings of 17.5 and a share of 27, but it continued good demographics: 53 men per 100 households watched; 75 women (with 50.2 aged 18 to 49); 34 teens and 57 children.[19] Numbers fluctuated every biweekly period, but generally these figures represented a decline in men and a steady holding of women, teens, and children compared with spring of 1974.

However, over the summer of 1975 several events occurred which produced an improvement in the numbers for *Happy*

Days during fall 1975 and led into the January 1976 premiere of *Laverne & Shirley*. Certainly a primary event was the institution of the family viewing hour which assisted the position of *Happy Days*. As discussed in the case of *All in the Family*, violence on television and its effects on children had been a preoccupation of the American public from the middle 1960s, culminating in the report of the National Commission on the Causes and Prevention of Violence in 1969 and then numerous social science studies funded by the federal government in the early 1970s. The FCC noted a jump in complaints about TV violence from around 2,500 in 1972 to 33,000 in 1973.[20]

Broadcasters' solution was a classic public relations one: they self-regulated, and agreed that from 7 P.M. to 9 P.M. Eastern time, no "adult-themed" shows would be programmed. The networks announced this remedy in April 1975, to start in the fall season. From the point of view of ABC, *Happy Days* looked like a valuable product since it was already doing at least adequately in its time slot against CBS's *Good Times* (another relevancy situation comedy spun off from *Maude*) and NBC's *Adam 12* (a police drama canceled at the end of spring 1975).[21] Moreover, it might do better against whatever its competitors chose to air in the more restrictive content climate.

The general effects of the new family viewing policy on the networks appeared not too dramatic in the first weeks; as of the week of 6 October 1975, Nielsens showed a 7 percent increase in young viewers and a 6 percent decline of adults. However, in the big picture, this was not too bad, and advertisers considered youth a valuable target audience. Moreover, the networks continued to introduce shows with violence into the later time period (and studies continued to indicate that Americans believed television offered too much violence).[22]

The family viewing hour was one factor improving the position of *Happy Days* in the fall of 1975; a second one was some minor reworking of its franchise. The stories go that Fred Silverman was a fundamental factor in the decision to make changes. After Silverman's success in helping Robert Wood turn CBS into a "relevant" network, ABC hired him in May 1975. Lawrence Bergreen writes that while at ABC Silverman tended to program to youth but with an "abundance of puerile sexuality," a "reliance on the habit theory of viewing," and a program choice that had a "general tenor of escapism."[23] It is the case that with the success of *Laverne & Shirley*, *Happy Days*, *Rich Man, Poor Man*, and other programs, ABC broke out of third place to number one in 1976. Whether those descriptors of Silverman's lineup are accurate is worthy of review.

At any rate, word came to the producers of *Happy Days* that Silverman wanted the character of Fonzie (played by Henry Winkler) emphasized. Although the original core of the program had been good boy Richie Cunningham (played by Howard), research indicated some popular interest growing in the "JD," Arthur Fonzarelli. Apparently school kids were beginning to imitate Fonzie's thumbs-up gesture and his phrase, "Aaaygh."[24] Moreover, ABC research conducted over the past season "concluded that viewers, finally through with Vietnam and Watergate, longed to return to traditional values."[25]

Beyond this, *Happy Days* director Jerry Paris also instigated another change: he talked producer Marshall into shifting from a one-camera filmed production mode to a three-camera film with a live studio audience. Originally Marshall had selected the one-camera format to evoke an "artistic, nostalgic texture" like that of *American Graffiti*, but Paris argued that concentrating on the new style and mode of shooting would permit him to devote attention to characterization and acting.[26] *Variety* commented on these announced changes in its opening-of-the-season review of *Happy Days*, and then sarcastically remarked: "The series is being done three-camera style before a live audience this year and apparently is taped in front of an audience of teenagers, judging from the squeals of delight on the soundtrack."[27]

These changes in character focus, dynamics, and shooting style produced a slightly altered *Happy Days* that also had a faster pace. Analysis of two episodes from the spring of 1974 versus three episodes from fall 1975 and spring 1977 illustrates the differences.[28] The third episode to air, "Richie's Cup Runneth Over" (29 January 1974), involves a typical teenage event—the first time becoming drunk. The narrative revolves around Richie's first look at dirty playing cards at a bachelor's party and his engagement in drinking games to the point that he has to be helped home by the nice "dancing girl" who entertained the men. In the final third of the episode, his father realizes he is drunk and helps him. Dad is fairly pragmatic about the situation, explaining the "spinning bed" phenomenon and helping him to the bathroom to throw up. Mom is somewhat naive, but understanding. Dad isn't angry or paternalistic; he points out that Richie has punished himself.

This episode's plot includes Potsie for whose cousin the party is given, but the dynamics of the episode centers on

Richie's learning experience. Fonzie appears in the episode as the "cool" guy on the bike from whom the less cool guys seek approval, and he already is displaying his thumbs-up gesture. However, he is not central to any of the plot's complications; he serves as mise-en-scène and exoticism. Cinematography is standard one-camera filming: "Richie's Cup Runneth Over" has one scene shot at night outside of Arnold's, the local teen hangout. Low lighting and good cinematography are evident; camera movements to follow characters are more than just pans and small tracking shots.

Another example from the first half year but toward the end of spring 1974 is "Knock Around the Clock" (air date 30 April 1974, episode 14)—a time when the series would have been operating somewhat routinely. In this episode, Potsie's bike is stolen by the Dukes, a tough gang that hangs out in the pool hall. Richie has just done a favor for the Dukes' leader, Frankie Molina, so he thinks if he just asks for the bike back, they will give it to him. Still Richie seeks help, and goes to Fonzie for advice. Fonzie's advice is to punch out the biggest guy first and the rest will scatter; Richie doesn't think he could do that. Richie asks dad, and dad says, don't go to the pool hall, but since Richie is an adult now, he can take the advice or not. Richie says he'll be back after he goes to the pool hall. At the pool hall confrontation, Richie, Ralph, and Potsie have mixed tactics. Potsie has tried to recruit the football team to back them, but it appears the team isn't coming. Meanwhile, Richie sticks to his nonviolence strategy, pointing out that now the world has the United Nations—there will be no more wars! Frankie is willing to give the bike back because of the favor he owes Richie, but then Frankie learns that Potsie has sent a note in which he threatened to beat badly the Dukes. The gang's honor is at stake, and a fight is about to occur when Fonzie and some of his friends arrive. The Dukes depart rather than mix with Fonzie's crew.

This episode continues to focus on Richie as an all-American boy and his typical teen experiences. Much more time is spent with Potsie and Ralph, although Fonzie's role is larger than before. Here Fonzie gives "cool" guy counsel—which Richie ignores, and then he saves the trio. Dad continues in his role as pragmatist and almost passive observer of Richie's teen troubles. Cinematography and editing are consistent with "Richie's Cup Runneth Over."

The three episodes from fall 1975 and spring 1977 show the changes occurring as a result of Silverman's directive and Paris's request. "Fearless Fonzie," airing 30 September 1975, is the forty-third episode and the fourth after the makeover. The opening shot centers on Richie, Potsie, and Ralph singing "All Shook Up," and Fonzie enters, to audience applause. Fonzie snaps his finger at one of the cute girls, but she says she's busy right now. Fonzie seeks Richie's private counsel—something is happening. He's losing his cool. Richie reassures him that he's just in a slump, like baseball players. But Fonzie recounts several other examples and then fails to start the jukebox by hitting it—a standard bit of character business that shows how transcendently cool he is.

The next scene opens with the Cunningham family watching a TV program, "You Wanted to See It." Fonzie appears, wearing a robe that "Mr. C" might wear (Fonzie has moved into the Cunninghams' garage apartment at the start of the season). Seizing an idea inspired by the show, Fonzie decides "he's back." He'll jump his bike over fourteen garbage cans on live television. Richie tries to talk him out of it, saying everyone knows Fonzie is cool. Fonzie doesn't have to prove it. Even if Fonzie is convinced of this, he also cannot go back on his word. He evokes examples of *High Noon* and looks to James Dean as his model. The episode ends with Fonzie midair over the garbage cans.

Part 2 of "Fearless Fonzie" involves the aftermath. Of course Fonzie survives, but he has two obstacles to face. First he has to have surgery on his knee, and then he has to start moving around even though it hurts. The latter problem is particularly bad because, as a result of the pain, he makes facial grimaces that aren't cool. In overcoming these hurdles, Fonzie seeks Richie's support. Richie tries to make him laugh in the hospital by wearing a "Groucho Marx" nose, glasses, and mustache. At home when Fonzie is recuperating much too long on the Cunningham couch, Richie brings in Fonzie's "A-list" of girlfriends. Fonzie's greatest concern is that he "look cool" and not be a "nerd." While he shows these insecurities to Richie, for Fonzie the importance of his external appearance is critical. This episode is particularly illuminating because the pattern occurs twice—both at the hospital and in the Cunningham living room. However, just in case the kids watching the program should not understand the message, the coda for the program shows the family and Fonzie watching a repeat of his jump. Fonzie declares, "I was a nerd to try that jump . . . but it was beautiful."

"A Shot in the Head," episode 88 airing during the spring of 1977, has much of the older narrative construction. In the opening scene, Richie comes into a basketball game with twenty seconds left on the clock and makes the winning shot. Enjoying his stardom during the week, Richie allows himself to be set up by the rival team for the next game. Using a cute girl as bait, they lure Richie to Arnold's and then plan to hold him there so that he will miss his game. Fonzie rescues him. However, when Richie arrives at the last minutes of the game and it is up to him to shoot a free throw that would tie the game and send it into overtime, he fails. In the final scene, his dad consoles him and reminds him that Richie was a hero for a week—longer than for many people.

What seems to develop over the course of the series is a strengthened focus on the relationship between Richie and Fonzie. At different times each saves and supports the other, but in very different ways. Richie's help comes through friendship; Fonzie's through "muscle" and street smarts. Additionally, both men move toward adulthood. Some of the more personal growth scenes—at least in these five episodes—involve Richie's reconciliations with reality. For Fonzie, the plot dynamics involve losing and regaining self-esteem. In that process, however, the audience is privileged to see a side of the "bad boy" Fonzie not glimpsed when he serves as a mere plot convenience—physical rescuer of Richie. The revelation, then, with both types of stories, is how adolescents can move toward adulthood.

This difference from the first season adds spice partially perhaps because of the tacitly voyeuristic appeal of seeing the "other" side of the world—how "cool" guys are also insecure. What focusing on Fonzie seems to provide the program is a bit more pizzazz. The shift in shooting style also perks up *Happy Days*.

As I mentioned, going to a three-camera style improved the pace of the episodes. This is certainly the case for the five episodes I sampled and analyzed. For the spring 1974 episodes, I counted the number of shots as 103 and 109 for the programs. Assuming a running time of about twenty-three minutes (a standard actual program time), the average shot length for the two episodes would be thirteen seconds. This is a fairly typical rate (compared with movies), but reasonable since sitcoms function around dialogue which produces shot/reverse shot shooting and editing patterns.[29] However, the three episodes from the 1975 and 1977 seasons run at 200, 142, and 148 total shots. The unusually high figure of 200 is due to a montage sequence showing everyone's tension as Fonzie prepares to leap the fourteen barrels, a scene that alone comprises 47 shots. If I eliminate that scene, and then average out the shots per episode, the shooting pace comes to 9.3 seconds, about 50 percent faster than the first season's sample. Camera movement continues, although mostly pans. In general, lighting is brighter since sets have to be lit so that shots from all three cameras will not produce unflattering shadows or obscured faces. Finally, the live studio audience produces a fuller sound track that actually seems more "credible" than the laugh track occasionally placed on the first season's episodes.

Whether these changes made a major difference is difficult to know, but by the middle of the fall, rating information indicated the program was beginning to inch up in the numbers. By the end of week 4, ending 5 October 1975, *Variety* reported that *Happy Days* and its follow-up in the Tuesday 8:30 P.M. time slot, *Welcome Back, Kotter*, had their best ratings yet for the season, although *Good Times* still beat *Happy Days* in its time slot. Moreover, Tuesday increasingly belonged to ABC, which already had Sunday night. By the end of October, *Happy Days* had tied with *Baretta* for number twenty-five, and its ratings were at 19.1 against 17.9 at a similar time the previous year. At the end of the fall season, *Happy Days* was nineteenth of seventy-eight programs, tying with *The Carol Burnett Show* at a rating of 21.3.[30] It was at this point that *Laverne & Shirley* premiered as a spin-off of *Happy Days*, with a guest appearance by Fonzie in the first two episodes, following its parent in the Tuesday night lineup.

The Reception of *Laverne & Shirley*

Laverne & Shirley had some similarities to its source, *Happy Days*.[31] In the premiere episode, Fonzie appeared as a friend of Laverne, played by Penny Marshall. It was a period piece—set in 1960. It was also set in Milwaukee, a typical Midwestern city. Unlike those of *Happy Days*, the main characters were single, working women who had been out of high school for some four years. Thus, instead of investigating the trauma of high school men and teenage dating, the program focused on the trauma of single, "career" women and young twenties dating, in 1960—a time of much greater sexual restrictions for women. At least, those were the most obvious dynamics of the series.

However, the first episodes indicated other features were at stake. For one thing, unlike for *Happy Days*, surrogate consumers perceived class as a crucial source for plot conflict. As

John J. O'Connor of the *New York Times* exclaimed in his review of the pilot/first episode, the program was a "surprise," "one of the best production efforts of the midseason sweepstakes." Although associating it with its lead-in of *Happy Days*, O'Connor wondered if "working-class white ethnic is big again." While he believed that "the working-class ethnics [appear] silly, the upper-class snobs are ridiculous and obnoxious. The series is playing the old, old game of sassy brashness devastating inhibited propriety." *Variety* also perceived this: "The wavelet of the near future on network tv appears to be proletarian comedy," and linked *Laverne & Shirley* to *The Honeymooners* and *All in the Family*. *TV Guide* and *Newsweek* followed suit.[32]

Indeed the first episode, "The Society Party" (27 January 1976), works on culture clash in a manner not dissimilar to that of *The Beverly Hillbillies* but with a bit more comeuppance to the rich. Laverne and Shirley are invited by the boss's son to a dinner at his home, not because he likes the women but because he wants to prove to his father that he has good relations with the workers. This motivation is quite apparent, and Laverne does not want to attend. Shirley convinces her to go, however, arguing that unless they mingle with those sorts of people they will never find eligible men in that class. She uses the song "High Hopes" to persuade Laverne. Laverne's hesitancy in part revolves around not having the right dresses to wear, so their friends Squiggy and Lenny secure gowns for them.

At the party, class differences are highlighted through exchanges between the women and the other guests, but mostly through obvious visual faux pax committed by Laverne. For example, she accidentally knocks off a statue's ear, and at dinner she tucks a napkin in her bosom. Then the crisis occurs: one of the guests recognizes Laverne's and Shirley's dresses as stolen from her daughters. Although Laverne and, especially, Shirley apologize and promise to return them on Monday, the woman continues her snipping. Laverne stands up, goes into another room dragging Shirley along, takes off the dress, returns in her slip and hands it to the woman. Stalking out of the room, Laverne says that the attack dogs treated them better. The program resolves itself with Laverne and Shirley reviewing their lessons. Laverne is the realist: Shirley's hopes are too high and Santa isn't going to give her a gentleman. Shirley counters, Laverne makes fun of everything and having high hopes is better.

One of the reasons Garry Marshall was approached originally by co-creators Miller and Milkus to develop *Happy Days* was that he was coming off the success of the TV version of *The Odd Couple*. *Happy Days* does not take up that dynamic in its stricter sense because the relationship between Richie and Fonzie does not function around personality conflicts. Instead, they take lessons from each other's worlds. However, *Laverne & Shirley*'s franchise is derived from the odd-couple formula. Two opposing personalities are put into the same apartment and work space; narrative conflict derives from the tussle between competing notions of how to resolve problems.

This system of plotting can be observed in two other examples of the first season of *Laverne & Shirley*. In the second episode, "The Bachelor Party" (airing 3 February 1976), the game is reversed. Now Laverne wants to do something and

Shirley resists. Laverne's father has requested that Laverne run his bowling alley for one evening. Fonzie needs a place for a bachelor party, and Laverne thinks that picking up the fifty dollars she'll earn will impress her father, who calls her "dopey" and who she thinks wanted a son instead of a daughter. Shirley is opposed to this because it is a bachelor party which will surely be a "palace of sin."

Naturally, things go wrong. They run out of pizza (not much comes of this plotline). The girl who was to pop out of the cake fails to arrive and only Shirley can fit into her costume. Fonzie fears that without a girl in a cake, the partygoers will trash the place. Shirley resists but finally agrees. A bit of visual fun occurs when she finally stands up and is wearing an old coat over the full-piece swimming suit outfit. As she starts to take off the coat, however, her boyfriend arrives and covers her with a tablecloth. Fonzie saves the place by moving the boys to bowling lane 12 for dirty movies. Resolution: Laverne owes Shirley for this, but Shirley did have an experience—a "disgusting experience." And Dad is pleased with the bonus money, calling Laverne "muffin," but ending with "dopey" for not having her shades pulled. Shirley helps her see the bright side.

"A Nun Story" (air date of 17 February 1976) works the same way. Shirley wants to keep having high school reunions. Laverne bursts her bubble by pointing out that no one is coming to them. However, with the expected appearance of Anne Marie, the possibilities of a lively time seem more likely. When Anne Marie arrives, however, Laverne and Shirley discover she has become a nun. This dampens the party until Laverne repeats an old joke that occurred when the three women had a slumber party. They had tricked Hector into walking into the room in his underwear; he repeats the entrance at the reunion. Shirley and Laverne are sure they have disgraced themselves in front of Anne Marie. As Shirley declares, it was the "most humiliating night of my life." Laverne talks her out of that attitude, and Anne Marie counsels that everyone should find what makes themselves happy without worrying about what others think.

This recounting of three of the early episodes of *Laverne & Shirley* indicates that while working-class ethnic topics do occur in the plots (but not consistently), surrogate consumers are able to perceive other aspects within the franchise. For one thing, beyond the odd-couple dynamic are the two women played by Penny Marshall and Cindy Williams. TV critic O'Connor specifically compared them to major women *film* stars: Barbara Stanwyck, Giulietta Masina, Lucille Ball, and Eve Arden. The *Los Angeles Times* declared them to be in the tradition of "slangy female slobs."[33]

This connection does not insure a positive evaluation. Cleveland Amory did not appreciate their "yelling" although he did like the sight gags. *Newsweek* reviewer Harry F. Waters had mixed reactions. The series "may sound terminally dumb" and "aiming at the 15-year-old mind," but it was gathering good ratings and its "uptight sexual tone seems as quaintly appealing as its cultural artifacts."[34]

The ratings were not just good, they were remarkable. The opening episode secured ratings of 35.1. Moreover, for the period of 19 January through 7 March 1976, *Laverne & Shirley* tied with *All in the Family* for first place with an average of 30.1. *Laverne & Shirley* also dragged *Happy*

Days up to number three with a rating of 28.5. Even more significantly, *Laverne & Shirley* assisted ABC's position. With one week left in the season, CBS led the networks by only 0.5, 19.5 to 19.0, and ABC—not NBC—was taking second place. Worse yet for CBS, ABC was winning the second season! Its rating average was 20.9 to CBS's 19.3; NBC followed at 16.9. ABC was taking Sunday, Monday, Tuesday, Wednesday, and Thursday nights. Of the top ten shows, eight were ABC's. Silverman's golden touch seemed to be working. *All in the Family* did take the 1975–76 year with an average of 30.1, but *Laverne & Shirley* ended third with 27.5 and *Happy Days* came in eleventh at 23.9. Second was ABC's *Rich Man, Poor Man* at 28.0.[35]

This success, and shift in TV dynamics, continued the following fall. A premiere-week special of *Happy Days* produced a rating of 34.7 and a 53 share; *All in the Family*'s special achieved ratings of only 27.3 and a share of 42. By the middle of fall, the transposition was obvious. ABC was leading the networks. *Happy Days* and *Laverne & Shirley* had taken an audience larger than the first hour of one of the World Series baseball games. The lead-in of *Happy Days* followed by *Laverne & Shirley* produced ratings in the low thirties; third-place *Charlie's Angels* (also ABC) was averaging 26.8.[36]

Demographics were good. For the period ending 1 January 1977, *Happy Days*' rating was 31.1 with a 46 share. Of 100 viewing households, watching were 58 men (40 in the age bracket of 18 to 49), 75 women (55 aged 18 to 49), 35 teens, and 63 children. The numbers for *Laverne & Shirley* were a rating of 30.0, share of 43; watching were 42 men

(36 between 18 and 49), 73 women (53 aged 18 to 49), 30 teens, and 60 children. These figures must also be considered comparatively. *Happy Days'* numbers for women aged 18 to 49, a most-favored group, were the highest for all network shows; *Laverne & Shirley* ranked second. For all women during the fall season, *Happy Days* and *Laverne & Shirley* averaged around sixth. For the same period for women 18 to 49, their average was third, but they secured first or second rank five times.[37]

For the 1976–77 year, *Happy Days* beat out *Laverne & Shirley* for the season, 31.5 to 30.9; trailing in third place was *ABC's Monday Night Movie* at 26.0. The following year *Laverne & Shirley* won with 31.6; *Happy Days* hit 31.4; and third was *Three's Company* (ABC). *Laverne & Shirley* managed to be number one for one more year (1978–79), with an average rating of 30.5. *Happy Days* dropped to fourth.

In retrospect, it is difficult to know quite what made *Laverne & Shirley* so popular and to what degree its programming pairing with *Happy Days* was critical in that success. While both series seemed aimed at adolescents, were certainly programs the whole family could watch, and were ones women in particular tuned in to view, formal analysis of their narrative dynamics yields many differences. Although critics initially did try to label *Laverne & Shirley* as just another nostalgic comedy—their key descriptors for the early *Happy Days*—the success of *Laverne & Shirley* forced further examination of the program. By the fall of 1976, writers focused on the similarity of the program with *I Love Lucy*. Others noted how rare it was to see the friendship of two women on TV, and Penny Marshall and Cindy Williams were praised for the sparkle between them (even as rumors began circulating about feuds on the set). Finally, slapstick and visual comedy had appeal. Introducing the fall 1978 season, *Variety* proclaimed that the premiere exemplified "the usual physical, knockabout-type comedy that Penny Marshall and Cindy Williams do so well, plus introducing a sentimental strain." These views are echoed by scholars who seek to explain the appeal of the series.[38]

The residual cultural and social effects of these programs range from parodies such as the takeoff of *Laverne & Shirley*'s opening credit scene in *Wayne's World* (1992) or the intertextual gesture of casting Winkler as the high school principal in *Scream* (1996) to more substantial consequences. As in the case of *All in the Family*, people were sensitive to what might be going on in learning behaviors. However, with *Happy Days*, the results seemed to be positive, especially when Fonzie was providing the right messages, for example, that jumping over fourteen barrels was the act of a nerd. As early as fall 1976, the press recognized the visible impact of the Fonz on clothing styles. Leather jackets were big, but tie-in merchandising helped support this effect. Fonzie's jacket went to the Smithsonian Institution in 1980, two years after the Bunkers' living room arrived.[39]

Better yet, according to the American Library Association, library card applications by children aged 9 to 14 increased by 500 percent after Fonzie signed up for a card and praised reading. A social science study in 1976 examined what adolescents were learning from *Happy Days*; the report card came back positive. While the youth declared they were learning to be "cool," they were also defining cool as discovering how to be inner-directed. How to do what they wanted to do rather than what others suggested was a major outcome.[40]

Of the four case studies, only that of *Happy Days* and *Laverne & Shirley* is an instance in which reworking a franchise likely made the difference in the program's eventual outcome. *The Beverly Hillbillies, All in the Family*, and *The Cosby Show* made adjustments to the program because of various factors, often involving the departure of a performer or the desire to refresh the writing. However, two of the programs started off with very strong ratings, and *All in the Family* captured the public's attention without compromising its design. Only in the case of *Happy Days* did an alteration make a difference.

This is not, however, to imply that reworking a structure will seldom produce higher ratings; in the history of television that has often happened. Rather, I note that ratings busters have basically been there from the start. Indeed, *Laverne & Shirley* started out in the top five and stayed there. While *Happy Days* was doing well and even improving in its numbers, *Laverne & Shirley* took it to the top. The coupled series then held those unusual ratings, to the envy of other programs, for several years before dropping back into normal rating numbers.

The case of *Laverne & Shirley* is also different from the other ones in one more way. Although cultural and industrial conditions can help explain its reception, more than for the other cases textual factors seem to be implicated in the mix. I am certainly not implying that the writing, plots, and performances of *The Beverly Hillbillies, All in the Family*, and *The Cosby Show* did not matter to their achievements. Rather, the normal critical explanation of cultural "nostalgia" for these two programs does not seem to be very pertinent. "Nostalgia" was dropped in fall 1975 to perk up the pace of *Happy Days* and to focus the comedy on Fonzie as well as Richie. Critics initially tried to label *Laverne & Shirley* as nostalgia, and then "proletariat comedy." Eventually, the features most pertinent and praised were the personal character dynamics and slapstick. A symptomatic reading of the series could potentially lead to deeper connections to American culture, but these would necessarily be much more ahistorical ones. Themes of class and ethnicity continue through all of these shows; interpersonal dynamics do as well. At any rate, factoring in the textuality, visual antics, and performances of *Happy Days* and *Laverne & Shirley* seems necessary to account for this case of a blockbuster sitcom.

[5]

The Cosby Show

In September 1984, *The Cosby Show* premiered. In hindsight, it is likely to be the last of television's prime-time programs to achieve a blockbuster audience. Clearly, in the future many programs will attract good numbers and good demographics, but the impact of cable and video and digital recording and playback permits late capitalism's dream: the segmented audience. Nielsen ratings over the summer of 1999 seldom showed network audiences exceeding ratings of 15. Dispersed across many channels, or popping in time-shifted or rented tapes or enjoying computer games, audiences have so much variety and choice that even media-hyped phenomena such as the final episode of *Seinfeld* or the live season premiere episode of *ER* will be only a brief blip in audience attention. Network television will likely still command space in social discourse. *Seinfeld* contributed greatly to our common casual language: "sponge-worthy," "the soup Nazi," and "master of your own domain" are understood—even if someone has not seen the program, just as we all know "round up the usual suspects," "make my day," and "the force be with you." However, even a very successful program may not be watched the evening of its initial broadcast. We are now post—prime time. I shall return to this point in the epilogue.[1]

The Cosby Show turns out to be the last program to secure some semblance of a cross-sectional, loyal audience, and it may have helped stave off the impact on the ratings of the new technologies for several years. Symptomatically, one of the programs—*The Simpsons*—to cut into the *Cosby* audience was from the upstart network FOX and was a show targeted to a very specific market segment.[2] Arriving on NBC's Thursday night lineup on 20 September 1984, *The Cosby Show*'s debut program achieved a rating of 21.6, and a 39 share. In its second season, *The Cosby Show* pulled "nearly half of the total television-viewing public." Moreover, it was top-rated with "kids, teens, adults under fifty-five, men, women, high- and low-income families."[3]

Such a success was not without controversy, however. Almost immediately, questions were raised about the social impact of the black family commanding this attention. The problem was not that the family members were black but that this black family was not like so many other black families previously seen on prime-time television. It did not fit stereotypes, and some critics questioned whether—even if this were a realistic representation of the upper middle class's experience in the United States—that representation was the most socially beneficial one to disseminate. This discussion has had no apparent outcome despite extensive critical and quantitative research.[4] Although the social implications of *The Cosby Show* are undetermined, its place within broadcast history remains prominent as one of the last broadly based, long-term, mass-media entertainment experiences created by television.

The Initial Reception of *The Cosby Show*

In terms of ratings, *The Cosby Show* started strong and then became stronger. The pilot episode secured a 21.6 rating and a 39 share for NBC, a network running third in the overall race for viewers. By the fourth week of its showing, *The Cosby Show* beat out the first half-hour of *Magnum, P.I.*, and, with a 21.3 rating, placed seventh in viewed programs for the period ending 21 October 1984. Number one was *Dynasty* for ABC with a rating of 26.3 and a share of 39.[5]

By late November, commentators noted that cable television and independent stations were continuing to eat away at the network audience. Only the sitcom, and especially *The Cosby Show*, was holding against this overall trend. At the end of the November sweeps, *The Cosby Show* had reached number one status with a 31.4 average and a 47 share. Other NBC sitcoms were also doing well—*Family Ties, Cheers,* and *Night Court* on Thursday nights were all in the top ten, and its hour-long dramas secured prestige for the network.[6]

If the statistics for the top programs for the 1980s are reviewed, the ultimate power of *The Cosby Show* becomes obvious. For the end of the 1984–85 season, *Dynasty, Dallas*, and *The Cosby Show* ranked one, two, and three. *Dynasty*'s annual average rating was 25.0—about in line with the ratings of top programs from the early 1980s on (see chart 1). The only variance in that period was the 1980–81 season rating of 34.5 for *Dallas*. In fact, the last time a top-rated program reached into the 30s was in 1978–79 when *Laverne & Shirley* secured a 30.5 and *Three's Company* had a 30.3. *The Cosby Show* came in third at 24.2 for its premiere season, but the next year it struck at the overall trend.

The Cosby Show achieved a 33.7 rating for 1985–86 and then a 34.9 for 1986–87. Its programming partner, *Family Ties,* also performed well. In 1985–86, *Family Ties* was second with a 30.0 rating, and in 1986–87 it was also second and up to 32.7. Equally noteworthy is that the third-place programs remained in the middle 20s. *Murder, She Wrote* ranked three at 25.3 in 1985–86; *Cheers* was third at 27.2 in 1986–87. In *The Cosby Show*'s fourth, fifth, and sixth seasons, its numbers declined to 27.8, then 25.8, and then 23.1. However, for two seasons, *The Cosby Show* defied the overall decline of audiences for prime-time network television.

Moreover, *The Cosby Show*'s demographics were broad. By the end of its first season, it was ranking as the top program for women 18 to 49, and estimates were that 90.4 women and 34.1 children per 100 viewing households were watching.[7] As usual, critical commentary turned to explaining the phenomenon. Three features became the core themes of discussion: the Huxtable family as a black middle-class family, the program's humor, and the fiction's realism.

One question frequently asked was whether *The Cosby Show* was contributing toward better images of minorities on television. The focus was not, however, on harmful stereotypes. Rather the debate was over whether the Huxtables were black. Some of the early publicity about the program stressed that *The Cosby Show* would be about parenting. The parents just happened to be black. Moreover, they just happened to be upper-middle-class blacks. One version of this was in the *New York Times*: "[T]he situation is the family, with an emphasis on the trials of modern-day parenthood." The rhetoric is more apparent in the *Hollywood Reporter*, quoting producer Tom Werner: "Cosby's universal theme of how we get through the day with our kids should appeal to a lot of people. He won't be just a black New Yorker, he'll be every father coping with every child."[8]

Picking up on the promotional language, *New York Times* critic John J. O'Connor praised the program, writing, "This particular family happens to be black but its lifestyle and problems are universal middle-class."[9] His crosstown colleague John Leonard, however, saw it another way:

The Cosby Show may be the best-written and best-acted new series of the merchandising season, but because it never gets out of the house it causes cabin fever. It is a sitcom throwback, atavistic in its yearnings: *Leave It to Beaver* in blackface.[10]

Leonard's remark about not leaving the house was a very perceptive one. For that was the complaint that other critics made. The problem with *The Cosby Show* was that it wasn't black enough. *Village Voice* critic Tom Carson wrote, "This family, quite determinedly, isn't black in anything but their skin color. I don't mean just in their lifestyle—even their cultural background, and their whole context of reference, is that of American Caucausians."[11]

The trouble with *The Cosby Show* was that it didn't show the day-to-day racism that existed in the streets of New York City for the Huxtable children. Oh, occasionally some inkling of the environment invaded the home. An early, first-season episode had Theo caught with a marijuana cigarette in his schoolbook, but his parents believed him when he said he didn't know how it came to be there. Cliff did remind him of their family policy on drugs: NO DRUGS. But the plot shifted from Theo in conflict over the decision of whether to bow to peer pressure to Theo anxious to prove to his parents that he wasn't lying.

It was this evasion of the exterior reality of black middle-class life that seemed most troublesome to some critics. Herman Gray discussed this as early as 1986, when he placed *The Cosby Show* in the early 1980s trend of "assimilationist" representations for blacks on TV. Gray defined the "assimilationist" view as one that "emphasizes core elements like individualism, racial invisibility, professional competence, success, upward social mobility and the routinization of racial issues." Absent were "representations of black collectivity . . . , racial conflict and struggle" as well as "black situations and viewpoints that provide different and competing alternatives to the dominant assimilation model."[12] Gray's list of assimilationist sitcoms included *Benson, Webster, Diff'rent Strokes*, and *The Jeffersons*.

What Gray was suggesting was not that issues of racism and lack of integration were not raised in some of these programs' episodes, but that the personal solutions naturalized the systemic, structural sources for the problems. It was the classic accusation of the mythical power of the American Dream. Indeed, as Thomas Cripps explained in his analysis of the controversy over an early black-cast TV series, *Amos 'n' Andy*, in the early 1950s, what was at stake—and likely a more difficult representational problem to resolve—was how to represent the black *middle class* when discrimination still existed.[13]

Leonard's criticism was scathing. He continued his essay:

> Once upon a time, before the neutron bomb, there was a nuclear family; our parents loved us wisely; therefore, we would never die. *M*A*S*H* dazzled the sitcom into sentience. . . .
>
> Nevertheless, tirelessly, Cosby reassures. Love goes on, even if it's black. Children get his message, especially if they're white. Cosby isn't dangerous, in the way that [Richard] Pryor and Eddie Murphy are, with their secret thoughts and seethings. Cosby bears no resentment; he won't hurt; he affirms; he's adorable. He won't talk to us like Jesse Jackson, and he won't be killed, like Martin Luther King. He sells Jell-O.[14]

Thus, not only was *The Cosby Show* not progressive, but it actually could create for whites the false impression that life was fine for blacks who worked hard. Its ideology was not just nonthreatening, it was deceptively reassuring.

However, just as *The Cosby Show* showed no alternative views from a critical white or black perspective, so too neither Leonard nor Gray spoke for all whites or blacks. As a middle-class (or better) black, Bill Cosby responded to the accusations that the program was "blackface" by arguing that not just whites had families; his "goal is to transcend questions of race, to concentrate on family life per se." Brian Winston argued, "Is it better that *The Cosby Show* in redressing some of the damage done by a long line of stereotypes, creates a spurious picture of black privilege?" That is, was realism the best representational solution after years of degrading images?

Additionally, black scholars and journalists were not sure how to evaluate the potential impact of this program, and often raised the problem only to leave it dangling. Eventually, this discussion turned to audience studies to attempt some partial answers.[15]

The debate over the implications of the representations in *The Cosby Show* did not produce the vitriolic discussion following the debut of *All in the Family*. Without a doubt this is because so much less was at stake. Presenting a blackface performance had nothing against the threat of making a white working-class male a "lovable bigot." *The Cosby Show* was also not aggressive in challenging taste cultures. In fact, the Huxtables were, if anything, too tasteful. Media commented in particular about the upsurge in sales of designer sweaters as a consequence of their conspicuous display in the Huxtable household.

If a taste culture was challenged, it was some presuppositions about what constituted the genre of sitcoms. A second line of discussion around *The Cosby Show* was what made it seem so different from other sitcoms. One explanation was the composition of its humor. Although I shall address the program's humor further below, here I want to note simply that public discourse perceived the program to be exceptionally low-key and different from the fare surrounding it. Instead of being a sequence of setups and put-downs (common to the genre, and especially to the other contemporary sitcoms featuring black characters), the program consisted of Cosby doing a comic routine—almost a stand-up number. Additionally, commentators suggested that the focus was on Cliff's (Cosby's) reactions to the circumstances. As O'Connor described it, "He does slow takes and delivers fast joke lines. He is on a roll and making the delightful most of it." Here Leonard agreed: Cosby "slow-takes and double-takes and cracks wise. He sidles and pounces."[16]

The humor might derive from comic routines or from exaggerated reactions to events, but it also harkened back to a formula to some degree eclipsed by the influence of *All in the Family*: the 1950s domestic sitcom. For Leonard to title his essay "Leave It to Cosby" and Carson to do this same with his "Cosby Knows Best" is telling. In fact, Carson argued,

So far as its premise goes, it's a throwback: the star's four kids do the darndest things, and he [Cliff] is sometimes comically exasperated but always ultimately wise and tolerant in his response to same. That's it. But this ur-formula may never have been handled with quite such relaxed bonhomie before; the humor accumulates as a set of small observations, which have been injected with just enough tang to keep the amiability short of being openly saccharine.[17]

Henry Jenkins argues in *What Made Pistachio Nuts?* that turn-of-the-century taste cultures privileged domestic wit over raucous slapstick, unsophisticated put-downs, and downright vulgarity; this differentiation was very much classbased.[18] *The Cosby Show* excelled in the former style, distinguishing itself from many of its TV competitors.[19] Thus, the very style of humor of *The Cosby Show* paralleled its white middle-class ambiance.

The third line of initial public discussion of *The Cosby Show* was associated with the question of novelty: this program seemed so realistic. As is usually the case with the use of the term *realism*, authors can mean various things. For *The*

Cosby Show, sometimes the meaning centered on recognizing situations in the program as true to everyday life. Another closely connected meaning was that it was possible to identify with the characters. A final meaning was that the program seemed visually or aurally to correspond to a notion of a real, empirical world. In almost every use of the term, however, this realism was constructed by opposition to the conventions of current TV sitcoms on the air in the mid-1980s.

Early publicity planted the use of the term *realism*. A preview story in the *New York Times* quoted coexecutive producer and head writer Earl Pomerantz as indicating that "[w]e wanted to show a real family in a real way." To expand on what this meant, he continued, "We think there's humor in just showing what parents go through with children, and what children go through with parents. More often what's shown is jokes; the rhythm of most shows is set-ups and punch lines. We're trying to find humor in the reality of the situation and the characters' attitudes toward each other." The article concluded by interviewing audience members after the taping of an episode and quoted one person as responding, "It was very realistic . . . I have six brothers and sisters, and I could definitely identify with the show."[20]

Both this verisimilitude of the situations and this sense of identifying with the characters are often repeated characteristics provided to explain the show's popularity, always in contrast to other sitcoms: "But 'The Cosby Show' is not just another family comedy. Unlike most such series, where contrived plots and rat-a-tat one-liners prevail, the Cosby series attempts to echo reality. It is filled with small moments that prompt chuckles of recognition in the viewer. The family is loving, but there is an edge as well: The children squabble, and the parents get exasperated." "Perhaps the series' most novel departure flows from its realistically bittersweet attitude toward parenting." And, the characters were "attractive and irritable rather than gimmicky and abrasive. The children in the show seem like real children instead of bit-sized adults."[21]

This break from the established conventions of the genre—constituted firmly by *All in the Family*—is, however, also one factor in opening up *The Cosby Show* to the criticism of avoiding external racial issues. The *Wall Street Journal* critic wrote:

> It's ironic that a formula that began by infusing social conflicts into the family should end up setting forth artificial families immune to social conflicts. . . . At least the Huxtable family seems real, not some formulaic device meant to teach the simple moral lessons inculcated by other television "situations" such as two black kids in the home of a white millionaire ("Diff'rent Strokes"), or a civil-rights activist raising the offspring of a reactionary police captain ("Gimme a Break").[22]

Thus, while the low-key humor and comedy based on situations or character flaws created an appearance of realism in contrast to the other sitcoms on television, that choice eliminated the hard-sell moralizing that accompanied the social relevance sitcoms.

I have argued that one explanation of the ratings buster is a cross-over effect. *The Cosby Show* is a useful example of polysemic appeal. It presented a cross-section of characters of all ages, providing places of identification for the audience segments most significant for networks and advertisers. Its middle-class tastes and style of humor corresponded to the "right" demographics. Its black characters permitted both a liberal response by whites (I can enjoy a show with black characters) and a set of positive images (or at least not offensive images) for black audiences. And all of this was set into narratives that did not threaten the middle-class status quo while promising the possibilities of the American myth to working people. It was, indeed, reassuring.

Verisimilitude, Humor, and Race in the *Cosby* Formula

The initial public discussion of *The Cosby Show*'s appeal invited an audience weary of "sex, violence, crime and greed in sitcoms"[23] into the safe Huxtable home. During the spring 1985 season, its episodes maintained the formula articulated by the show's producers as the ratings steadily climbed. In some sense, the first descriptions of the program were quite accurate in conveying significant features of the formula. However, in the debates over the possible social implications of the show, little work was done in verifying or expanding upon the early perceptions of the program's characteristics. Much of the public discourse was also around Bill Cosby as a real person. Was he actually someone not quite as amiable as the character he portrayed in the program? Why was he so caustic with some reporters and, occasionally, quite egotistical?

But the discourses around social obligations and Cosby-as-star seem to have existed in another realm from the interests of the television consumer. Certainly, neither set of discussions produced any reduction in viewing. Apparently consumers were willing to tune into the program, if not loyally, at least in larger numbers than sitcoms had been experiencing for some time.

To consider what the *Cosby* formula provided them, I have analyzed eight episodes which premiered from 31 January through 2 May 1985.[24] These account for most of the program's second half-season while it was reinforcing its initial popularity. I also examined briefly several episodes of other contemporaneous shows starring black characters. I must admit that at times when I was watching *The Cosby Show* I thought I might be viewing *Sesame Street* or *Mr. Rogers' Neighborhood*, except for short scenes in which Cliff and Clair's sexual enjoyment in each other took the program into 1980s prime time. Several features typified *The Cosby Show* formula in this first season. One was the handling of the gestures and movements of the characters. Another was the humor construction. The third was the resolution of the narrative "problems."

Especially in contrast to other domestic sitcoms of the early 1980s, *The Cosby Show* was remarkable in its naturalistic directing of the characters' physical movements. When children come into the kitchen, they don't sit in the chairs. They plop down into them, and hit the table. When the youngest child, Rudy, won't eat her brussels sprouts, she hangs over the edge of the table, playing with the food. But more striking is that the family affectionately touches each other. Dad puts his arms around the children, and he kisses the kids. Scarcely an episode exists in which this is not a part of at least one scene.

I want to stress here that this physical affection is not scripted as a reward for good behavior. That is, it does not come as part of a positive climax ("kiss and make up"). Rather the touching and hugging accompany even the most routine parts of life, such as making a bed. This underlying physicality provides, I think, part of both the realism and the reassurance permeating the program. Parents may require you to make the bed but they are hugging you while they do it.

A second characteristic of *The Cosby Show*'s formula was how it constructed humor. As I discussed, other prime-time situation comedies of the period often constructed their humor on the basis of sarcastic put-downs of characters (one-liners) or misunderstandings among the characters that produce dramatic tension. For example, in a sampled episode of *The Jeffersons*, Louise learns that George is suffering from ulcers, so she does everything she can to prevent him from being aggravated. The consequence is that she avoids the normal sarcasms directed by most of the characters in the program toward each other until she finally explodes as a result of her mother-in-law's belittling of her. The resolution, however, is that George actually thrives on some types of work stimulation from which she thought he needed to be protected. Or in a sampled episode of *Diff'rent Strokes* the siblings tease each other, providing much of the joking. The story's structure relies on the audience's knowledge that the children are going to decoy dad out of the house so that the older boy, Willis, can have sex with his girlfriend for the first time.

Both of these comedic strategies are long-standing in the sitcom genre. One-liners and sarcasm are efficient from a production stance: characters stand there and insult one another. This does not take a lot of set construction or multiple camera setups. Comedy deriving from misunderstandings is also economically advantageous since it also thrives on letting the audience know more than some of the characters.

If these types of humor construction are normative within the sitcom genre, *The Cosby Show* deviated in its methods of humor while still remaining low-cost. Comedy in *The Cosby Show* centered on character foibles. Harkening back to the "quality" television style of *The Mary Tyler Moore Show*, and forecasting to some extent the warmedies and dramadies of the second half of the 1980s and the 1990s,[25] *The Cosby Show* relied on the ambivalence of humanity to create recognition of the good and the "lovable" in each of us. This type of comedy worked well for Cosby as a performer since the humor came from "within" the person upon which the situation was focusing. Cosby as the dad was positioned to be the focus of the sitcom; he was also the privileged performer and the central figure for identification.

Thus, Rudy may not know how good brussel sprouts are—at least *for* her. Denise may think she's more adult than she is. Vanessa may need to learn that she should not blame others for her shortcomings. Theo may need to be careful about who his friends are. Who will teach them all of this? Dad, as the benevolent authority in the household. Dad, however, thinks at times that he is a better teacher than he is. Denise is the person who gets Rudy to eat her brussel sprouts. Denise finds out from her friends that not only she has parents who think staying out all night to buy tickets to a concert is unwise. With dad's coaching, Vanessa articulates her own lesson—she shouldn't blame others. Theo already knows the lesson; dad just needs to be reassured of that fact.

In this discussion of the textual ambivalence around the figure of the dad, however, I do not mean to imply that *The Cosby Show* belittled its central character or became ironic (especially given that Cosby is exceptionally proud of his doctoral degree in education). In fact, many of the episodes used the strategy of making Cliff partially fallible just to elevate him as the wise but subtle teacher. Dad may invariably attempt to fix broken machines around the house but inevitably fail at this job. Dad may need to get back into shape to run a race against his old college nemesis. Dad may be surprised that his friend has a very young girlfriend. However, dad is also able to entertain eight small children at Rudy's slumber party. Dad can enlist the team effort of the Huxtable children to take care of the house when Claire has an important case. Dad also has already secured the respect of Theo who is anxious not to fall in dad's esteem. Dad's faults are minor compared with his virtues.

The use of character foibles as the central comedic strategy also permits visual focus on Cosby. Commanding the screen, Cosby's reactions become both the cue for how we should react to the events and the source of our own amusement. The structures of identification nearly rhythmically circulate from the characters who interact with Cliff to Cliff himself. Not all episodes work this way, but many do.[26]

The egotism of this would perhaps be more grating if the stakes were higher. As I have implied, in this sitcom very little really is significant—in the broader scheme of life events. *The Jeffersons* and *Diff'rent Strokes* discuss ulcers and teen sex. *The Cosby Show* presents lessons about how to entertain at slumber parties—line the kids up on the couch and play "kids say the darndest things." Thus, the narrative stakes are reduced to the inconsequential, and Cliff's foibles (which are already less significant than his assets) become enjoyable rather than irritating or dangerous (which was not the case for the early Archie Bunker).

Using character foibles as the site of the construction of humor harmonizes well with the way narrative trajectories operate. Mark Crispin Miller accuses *The Cosby Show* of being a show about nothing: "*The Cosby Show* is devoid of any dramatic tension whatsoever. Nothing happens, nothing changes, there is no suspense or ambiguity or disappointment."[27] Miller is wrong. Things do happen in *The Cosby Show*, but they are not the things commonly associated with comedy built on sarcasm or misunderstandings.[28]

In the eight episodes analyzed for this study, fifteen plot problems exist. Although some episodes have only one problem, others have three, with an overall average of two. The problems range from the trivial—Rudy won't eat her brussels sprouts and Cliff needs a babysitter—to the most serious one of a young neighborhood boy in trouble. Resolutions occur in every case but often so quietly as compared with the usual heavy-handed sitcom style that they are unnoticed. Rudy does eat her brussels sprouts when Denise tells her that Rudy can watch Denise and her friends dance as soon as she finishes her vegetables. Cliff finds his babysitter by telling Theo that it's his job. Theo doesn't argue, so no complications arise. The neighborhood boy is helped by the community center directors, who simply let him know they will be available to him when he wants.

Interestingly, the resolutions usually occur through two

devices. One is an exchange or reward system, or—in a negative form—bribery. Besides the brussels sprouts example, Denise is allowed to have her friends over to dance rather than stay out all night to buy concert tickets; Theo must babysit because that's his job as a member of the household; Cliff may try to fix a machine if he will buy a new one if he isn't able to repair it; the children must keep the house clean if they don't want it to be a mess; Cliff ties a race after working out hard; Rudy has a slumber party when she can't go skating with Vanessa; and the children receive a dollar if they will remain quiet. Some of these rewards, exchanges, or bribes have a potential for a violent outcome should the deal not be accepted by the other party. However, refusal does not appear to be a reasonable option because either the reward is too good or refusal too dangerous.

The second device for narrative resolution is talking about problems among family members (mostly between Cliff and someone else). The marijuana joint in Theo's book, Theo's need to prove to his dad that he is not involved in drugs, Vanessa's ability to succeed in a new science class, Vanessa's need to learn where to place blame, Cliff's unease with his friend's new girlfriend, and the small boy's troubles are all dealt with through conversations about actions and feelings. These conversations invoke demands of self-responsibility, and they rely on an underpinning theory that talk will clear away difficulties.

Such a method of resolution is fairly evident even though it is not specifically discussed in the episode itself. That is, the examples are presented, but no character says, "Talk will resolve family disputes or personal failings." This low-key approach to resolving narrative problems as well as the comparatively insignificant issues—insignificant relative to the rest of television's issues—explains why Miller thinks nothing is happening. Indeed, compared with the rest of prime time (and the front pages), nothing is happening. Yet compared with *Sesame Street* and *Mr. Rogers' Neighborhood,* much is going on and of a very similar nature.

The Cosby Show functioned as the lead-in on NBC's Thursday night prime time. It attracted children and women but other constituencies as well. Its overall style of humor and resolution of narrative problems matched Middle America's taste standards and contemporary views about responsible parenting. Despite the possible negative ideological and social effects of such a "reassuring" program, its features and its differences struck its viewers as refreshing. For at least a of couple years, *The Cosby Show* functioned nationally as a ratings buster and a common social experience of the sort created by *The Beverly Hillbillies, All in the Family,* and *Laverne & Shirley.*

Epilogue: Some Final Observations

At the beginning of chapter 1, I noted that Sigmund Freud believed that two reasons existed to study jokes: one was that all mental happenings are connected, the other that a joke passes from person to person like the "news of the latest victory." Reasons to understand the very popular (and not popular) television sitcom seem the same. Whether the very popular, blockbuster series takes a while to build or whether it starts off very strong and then becomes even stronger, public discussion has to be a major part of what attracts the audience's attention and eventually focuses it on that program. Surrogate consumers in the forms of publicity machines from the networks, critical response in the paper, and public discussion around a series help carry the news to the potential audience. Yet the audiences themselves also form "news" that goes back to the critics and networks in the shape of Nielsen ratings, audience analysis, news stories, and ad hoc observations.

Why some types of humor and joking captivate major segments of the population at particular times is *not* answered by this study. Yet, I would argue that this study does suggest generalizations about both what has not been consistent among the blockbusters series and what has been.

One of the variables for these sitcoms is the type of humor, comedy, or joke structure. As I have discussed, the comedy in *The Beverly Hillbillies* works through puns and situational misunderstandings created by cultural differences between the Clampetts and Beverly Hills people. *All in the Family*, however, operates via tendentious joke structures in which Archie is generally the butt of the joke. (I would predict that a study surveying individuals aligned with Archie versus those associating themselves with Michael would produce conclusions that the jokes were in radically different places.) *Laverne & Shirley* and *The Cosby Show* use visual reactions by characters and situational misunderstandings among family members or friends for their major comic address. Comedic identification operates differently for these two programs: for *Laverne & Shirley*, identification by the viewer with the characters should produce embarrassment and reconciliation; for *The Cosby Show*, the response solicited by the text is usually empathic recognition.

The humor, comedy, and joking are both character- and situation-based for the programs, but the franchises treat their characters quite differently. While character transformation is a sensitive decision for producers (changing characters will invariably alter the situational play—see the case of *Happy Days*), it is easier to tinker with minor characters than major ones. Thus, Edith becomes less of a dingbat over the course of the show, and her departure provoked a heightening of the "lovable" features of Archie. The Huxtable children also develop both in complexity and personality through the series. In general, however, the other main characters remain fairly consistent through the series.

Character causality is also variable among the programs. In *The Beverly Hillbillies*, *All in the Family*, and *Laverne & Shirley* several individuals may take actions which will catch up other characters in the situations. However, although this nonfocused agency is possible in *The Cosby Show*, the plot impact of the events all center on Cliff's response; thus, everyone else in the show becomes a subsidiary character within a hierarchy rather than an ensemble such as exists in the other three programs.

The degree of verisimilitude among the programs differs as well. Both *The Beverly Hillbillies* and *Laverne & Shirley* start plots off with credible premises but delight in taking those foundations to absurd conclusions through heightening misunderstandings. (I always have the desire to say to the characters that they just need to talk to each other and everything would be clarified—but, of course, there would go the plot!) *All in the Family* and *The Cosby Show* use the everyday as the basis for working around and through common family interactions. Always grounded in the real, these programs investigate the consequences of disjunction but seldom if ever become surreal, as is usually the case for *The Beverly Hillbillies* and *Laverne & Shirley*.

The question of comedic, character, and verisimilitude structures and of the types of emotional responses as a reaction to those structures introduces the difficult textual hypothesis about address and ideology. In the ideal response (from the point of view of the text) to these programs, what would likely be the ideological position for the viewer? I would suggest that for all four of the programs, audiences presumably operate conservatively. That is, the programs solicit from the knowledgeable and cooperative viewer a maintenance of the values held coming into the program. The series do not try to convert viewers to new sets of values so much as solicit agreement where sympathies already exist.

Now what those established values are already should also

be ideologically analyzed. Here, audience reception studies are really necessary to speculate about interpretations of the programs. The case of *All in the Family* is easy to predict. For instance, alignment with Archie would produce a very different audience view about the issues at stake in the text than alignment with Michael. However, readings of *The Beverly Hillbillies* might be similarly complex. Do the Clampetts stand for traditional family ways, or might they also be read as supporting natural behavior and respect for everyone as equals? Could the Clampetts be complicit with the forthcoming hippie generation? Either seems possible, and without reception analysis, we will not be in a position to make any generalizations about the ideological and cultural implications of these programs.

While the four blockbuster sitcoms differ in comedic structure, character, verisimilitude and address, some common features do flow through the various sitcoms that have been ratings busters. For one thing, the four programs all seem to raise issues about class through discussions of conflict between classes or examples of social mobility. *The Beverly Hillbillies* starts this trend through its humorous analysis of the disjunction between values; *Laverne & Shirley* (much more than *Happy Days*) overtly displays the disparities between economic groups. The debates among the members of the Bunker household hinge on a display of the anxieties of a white working-class male situated within a world of shifting privileges. Even the Huxtables become an exotic display of the "unknown" class in American culture: the black professional who has succeeded.

These class issues are often obscured by humorous jokes or

situations that foreground taste or personal or generational preferences. That is, recognizing that these series are raising class (and ethnic/race) problems can be avoided if all that seems at stake are lifestyle choices rather than structurally embedded differences within America. Thus, it is very suggestive that three of the programs present elitist white culture (Beverly Hills people, snotty Milwaukee socialites, even at times Michael Stivic as an upwardly mobile ethnic)[1] as the butt of much aggressive joking. This foregrounding of lifestyle (read class, ethnic/race) conflict does not occur explicitly in *The Cosby Show*, but that program offers its critique by inclusion of the other. In the episodes analyzed, break dancing, swing, and jazz are black musical cultures offered to the audience. Additionally, throughout the series the writings and visual arts of the Harlem Renaissance and African American artists are evident and even foci of a couple of plot problems.[2]

This implicit foundation in class and ethnic/race variations may be involved in the four programs' wide appeal to multiple audience groups. Nielsen data are not available to study consumer income levels for the various audiences, but this information would be very meaningful in coming to terms with the blockbuster phenomenon. Throughout the history of prime time, individuals with higher incomes were less likely to use network television for entertainment simply because their wealth gave them more flexibility for choosing media sources. Hence, statistics indicate that children and ethnic minorities on the lower end of the economic spectrum are higher users of free TV. Although (basically) equally available to everyone in the United States, network TV has not been equally used. I shall return to this below in a discussion of the postnetwork era. Here it seems sufficient to indicate that the blockbuster phenomenon may have a complex relation to class and ethnic/race disparities.

A second similarity among the "must-see" series is that they are about extended, multigenerational families, and they are primarily domestic comedies rather than comedies of the workplace as family. *The Beverly Hillbillies* offers a three-generation household with goals and aspirations for the youngest members of the group that provide the inciting incident for the series: they need to go to Hollywood so that the youngsters have better opportunities for careers and marriages. *All in the Family* starts off with a two-generation household, with the presence of the son-in-law intensifying the intergenerational conflicts. *The Cosby Show* also routinely displays the multiple generations of the Huxtables, eventually showing four, when one of the daughters has twin babies they name Nelson and Winnie. The Cunninghams "adopt" Fonzie, but even without him, the series is about children growing up. Only *Laverne & Shirley* might be said to be a questionable inclusion within this generalization. However, if you consider the two as an "odd couple," then they fit this pattern. Certainly Laverne's interest in making her father proud is important for some plots.

Beyond the lifestyle and generational focuses which together permitted the class and ethnic/racial stakes to exist implicitly, every series was perceived in its time as refreshing the genre. As observers of television who have access to these programs without historical context, this novelty factor is sometimes difficult for us to imagine. Yet, *The Beverly Hillbillies* and *Laverne & Shirley* seemed to their contemporaries to be quite socially perceptive. Certainly *All in the Family* was. Even *The Cosby Show* appeared "realistic" in contrast to its competition, and audiences found this innovative.

Finally, the programs offered numerous pathways of pleasure into the narratives or viewing experiences. Apparently unanticipated by the producers, *All in the Family* provided the most variable avenues. Descriptions of viewers and debates around the program indicate that several identification opportunities existed. While as a radical, I would not like to have people usually identify with Archie, still significant evidence exists to indicate that this occurred for many viewers. The other programs are more closed off. While several people exist with which to identify (fathers, mothers, sons, and daughters), the general side the audience should take in any plot conflict is much clearer. The programs do not encourage us to imitate or approve the actions of the upper classes in *The Beverly Hillbillies* or *Laverne & Shirley*. To an almost too sweet level, audiences are pleaded with to associate themselves with Cliff Huxtable. The comedic request is a laughter of empathy.

Polysemy does exist as it must for any text, but I believe that the multiple-generation property of these sitcoms is a more significant factor than character identification in providing opportunities for audience engagement with the programs. The series star several individuals, and identification is possible with any of these featured characters. However, the ratings-buster sitcoms differ from many less successful sitcoms in that almost none of the characters are presented as having significant flaws. All failings are of a minor nature. This is the case even for Archie, who is consistently and anxiously described as a "lovable bigot." This feature is normal for the domestic sitcom, although it is not the case for some comedies structured around the workplace or friendships. These other sitcoms may have many characters like these domestic sitcoms, but avenues of association are limited, with one or two central figures becoming the comedic focal point. I think here of *The Mary Tyler Moore Show*, *M*A*S*H*, *Cheers*, and *Seinfeld*—all favorite programs of many of my colleagues in academia. Mary, perhaps Lou Grant, and Hawkeye might be figures for identification, but most of the rest of the casts operate as objects for comedic situations. Consider it this way: does *Cheers* really ask you to identify with Sam as *The Cosby Show* requests your alignment with Cliff? Is George, Kramer, Jerry, or Elaine a figure for role-modeling?

Pleasure in these blockbuster programs, moreover, does not seem to be limited to identificatory fantasies. As I noted in chapter 1, Patricia Mellencamp's remarks about the pleasures of watching performances are worthy of much further research. Although it is only critical response that I have available to me, the period commentators on these programs often remarked with delight about the enjoyment they had watching the actors act. Although these programs were usually filmed, or filmed before a live audience, the speed of producing sitcoms for weekly television requires an "onstage" mix that either jells or doesn't. Likely good writers, directors, and production teams make opportunities for the actors; thus, the "chemistry" on a set isn't due just to the craft of the stars. Together, though, sometimes the performance combinations work, and sometimes they fall flat.

The difficulty of describing or analyzing this feature of a media text is notorious. All I can say is that when I watch these programs I seem to sense that the people making them are enjoying the process themselves. They are engaged and not just walking through their lines.

Everyone would like to create the next ratings buster. The options, however, seem limited to a palette with a set number of colors that are simply available for recombination and blending. A 1995 *New York Times* essay set out charts for the various contemporaneous options. For the "young single professional" lead character, programs chose looking for love or looking for success, in pairs or in packs, with rotten love lives or with rotten love lives until now, in some big or small city. The "young divorced professional" might have rotten a love life (mostly), with children (mostly), with one or more meddling parents, and possible forced contact with an ex-spouse.[3]

This apparently limited set of parameters has itself fed into the comedic realm. A classic humorous gambit is to mix generic types. For example, "Buried with Children" is a "zombie sitcom." Or in Mike Peters's "Mother Goose and Grim," the dog Grim watches television, with the following dialogue coming from him: "This is a new record. I've watched 18 hours of straight television. Who says I'm not a watch dog? Oh, oh, this week Jed Clampett and Jethro were caught peeping in the girls locker room. . . . Ellie May says she's hooked on diet pills. . . . And Granny starts wearing thong bikinis. I never miss *Beverly Hillbillies 90210.*"[4]

The one obvious conclusion that can be drawn from these examples is that in all cases the ratings-busting program altered the character of prime-time television. In each case, spin-offs and imitators attempted to offer to audiences what appeared to be engaging them. Many imitators were very successful; one even became a ratings buster and revolution itself. Yet, many imitators looked just like what they were: copies of something else.

The reason that imitation often functions well in television, however, is the reason why a ratings buster is so successful. Audiences may want the genre refreshed from time to time. However, they also come to the program because they know what it will give them. The promise of repetition of the pleasure from last week is why the set is turned on to the particular channel at a specific time. That familiarity is crucial in selling the vast majority of entertainment. That it works for prime-time television is scarcely an outstanding observation. Yet this point does need to be made. Each of these programs offered a formula that became expected and routine, and to have deviated significantly from the formula would have broken the contract with the audience. Here, again, an opportunity for theorizing the pleasure of prime-time television exists. For it is not merely the pleasures of identification and observation of performances that these shows offer but the pleasures of a repetitive fantasy structure. I have sketched some aspects of each of these programs in terms of a symptomatic reading of their individual mise-en-scènes of desire as they relate to class and diversity issues. However, this book is charged not with speculating about audience reception but rather with considering the institutional dynamics involved in the public reception of these situation comedies. Still, eventually, another work should consider (once again) the dynamics of humor, comedy, and jokes employed within the half-hour dramatic narrative form for groups of audiences and individuals. Such a reception study of "must-see-TV" matters.

Why does it matter? Although I have mentioned two obvious cultural impacts such programs have—the invention of catchphrases and the stimulation of interpersonal community exchange the days after a program—these are but symptoms of something much deeper culturally and socially. Blockbuster and other successful television programs become our memory of our childhood and adult lives, of our nation and its generational growth. The fact that our public memory has focused on *Father Knows Best* and *Leave It to Beaver* as representative of the late fifties and *All in the Family* as the early seventies and that most people currently have no idea how widely watched were *The Beverly Hillbillies* and *Laverne & Shirley* is terribly significant for thinking about how we as a large group of people remember and forget, and how films and television programs are signally part of our construction of our imagined present and past.

This issue of the cultural influence and heritage of blockbuster sitcoms is even more on the agenda as we move out of the network era and into post-prime time. Here it is important to consider the cultural effects of changing delivery circumstances in relation to the phenomenon of typical versus blockbuster viewing.

In the late 1970s, general viewership of the three networks was approximately 90 percent. That is, if you were watching television, you were likely watching one of the three networks. However, this was about to change. One factor was the diffusion of home video cassette recorders. In 1982, 4 percent of all TV households had VCRs; in 1988, 60 percent did.

Moreover, 21 percent had at least two! Furthermore, these owners used their machines. A survey in early 1988 indicated that in a VCR household, people recorded 179 minutes (almost 3 hours) and watched 296 minutes (almost 5 hours) of recordings per week. Video tape rentals were at 2.3 cassettes per month. Remote controls may have facilitated this since they were used to zap commercials as well as shift channels. A second technological change was the spread of cable (and satellite) delivery of programming. In 1978, 17.1 percent of households had cable; in 1989, the figure was 57.1 percent. Thus, over the same period as the diffusion of VCRs, cable access accelerated similarly into television households. By 1991, the percentage of U.S. homes wired for cable was over 90 percent even if only about 60 percent of households were subscribing to services.[5]

The effects of these technological changes were hardly startling: viewership of the three networks declined from a 90 share in 1979–80 to a 67 share in 1988–89, and to less than 60 percent by 1991. The figure has been decreasing since, especially as FOX, Lifetime, Warner Bros. Television, and other niche networks are increasingly drawing viewers from the full-service networks and as pay channels are providing original series and movies.[6]

Beyond noting the shifting of audience shares away from the big three networks, studies also consider viewing behaviors. A 1988 analysis discovered that age, sex, and income bracket were differentials in how television was viewed. Statistics indicated that men usually watched more channels than women by a figure of 8.5 channels to 7.8. People in the age bracket of 25 to 34 usually watched 10 channels, while lowest in the variable age brackets were people 65 and older who typically stuck with 5.7 channels. Income showed differences too. Those people in households making more than $30,000 watched 9.7 channels, compared with 7.2 channels for those earning less than $30,000.[7]

These demographic differences are also played out in the markers of ethnicity and race. Observers have been aware for some time that black audiences watch more television per person than do white audiences. For instance, in 1988 black households watched television 10.6 hours daily while other groups averaged 7.3 hours. Blacks were more loyal to the big three networks which did not discourage their attention since U.S. blacks' income made them as a group "wealthier and more populated than most nation-states in the world." Moreover, as J. Fred MacDonald points out, black preferences could tilt overall ratings. In a study of the impact of black viewership on Nielsen ratings for early 1986, MacDonald shows how strong black viewership could produce variance in final ratings and ranks of programs. For instance, while *A Different World* secured a 22.4 rating and number four rank for nonblack viewers, its 46.6 rating and number one rank with blacks resulted in a 25.0 final rating and number two rank. Similarly, black audiences brought *227* from a rank of 31 to an overall rank of 22.[8]

The racial disparity in viewing preferences noted by the *New York Times* in December 1998 was equally present in 1986.[9] While both black and nonblack viewers ranked *The Cosby Show* number one, black audiences ranked *227* number four and *The Facts of Life* number six, while nonblack audiences ranked them sixteenth and twenty-sixth. Conversely, nonblack viewers considered as their third-ranked program *Murder, She Wrote* and fourth-ranked *60 Minutes* against black audiences' rankings of 25 and 32 for those shows. In 1998 the top shows for blacks were the *Steve Harvey Show* (on the WB network, ranked number one) and the *Jamie Foxx Show* (WB, ranked number 2). White viewers ranked these two programs 118 and 124, respectively. Meanwhile, *E.R.* was ranked number one with white viewers while blacks ranked it fifteenth. As the *Times* article indicated, this is a "racial divide" that will likely only grow as channels multiply and targeting specific audiences by niche networks becomes entrenched.

What do these delivery changes and niche appeals mean for the blockbuster phenomenon? First, that a ratings buster of the sort I have described is unlikely to occur ever again. With average ratings dropping into the low teens, if that, achieving a ratings buster won't happen because too much choice is available. Now, a 3.5 rating for shows such as *Felicity* is considered adequate to achieve program renewal. Second, consequently, accessing broad variable segments of the U.S. population will not occur. Rather, specific types of audiences will be reached.

The elimination of blockbusters will *not,* however, necessarily result in a decline in the function of television as the production site of our cultural present and past. Two factors prevent that. One is that the programs watched by today's youth will likely serve as their touchstones for their experiences as they move into their roles as cultural producers in some ten to fifteen years. Like it or not, *Beavis and Butthead* and *South Park* may be future markers of the 1990s if it is their viewers that become the culture creators. It might well be worth tracking youth preferences now to study how history will be written later.

Second, even though most television programs may not be watched in large numbers, the mass media that mark out trends and the remote control may override the decline in habitual and mass viewing. *Ally McBeal* has only routine ratings, but likely almost every American knows something about the main female character from either scanning through the program or news sources. The story of whether the lead actress, Calista Flockhart, has an eating disorder has graced the cover of numerous periodicals, been discussed in interview shows, and been the subject of jokes on late-night TV. Ally's short skirts were the subject of a "life & arts" feature of the *Austin American-Statesman,* which talked a local woman attorney into wearing an "Ally-length outfit" to court for a day.

The study of the cultural implications of the blockbuster television program, thus, requires at least a two-pronged attack. One strategy is to search out how groups of individuals interpreted and used the programs in their daily lives and, eventually, their memory. The second strategy is to consider the post hoc construction of the past by groups who may have the cultural power to suggest that some programs "represent" eras. As I have mentioned in the preface to this book, whenever I have discussed this research project, I have enjoyed quizzing my auditors. I ask them to speculate which programs were the blockbusters. I wish now that I had kept better records on responses. Not surprisingly, answers by television scholars and academics in general tend to edge toward sitcoms categorized as "quality" television—

The Mary Tyler Moore Show, *M*A*S*H*, and similar shows. Surprise usually greets me when I explain that one of the ratings busters was *The Beverly Hillbillies*. I can just see taste cultures interfering with my quiz respondents. (*Laverne & Shirley* is usually greeted with a knowing nod by younger academics who often seem less inhibited by notions of high and low taste than older scholars.) Thus, while this study has focused on institutional dynamics, public discourse, and media theory to account for the phenomenon of must-see TV, the project only sets the stage for further research about reception and cultural studies.

Notes

NOTES TO THE PREFACE

1. The interpretations of *Dallas* by various groupings of people have been widely studied, but how its sudden popularity after two years on the air was initially discussed and how that interplayed with network and textual features could be examined.

2. Michele Hilmes, *Hollywood and Broadcasting: From Radio to Cable* (Urbana, IL: University of Illinois Press, 1990); Christopher Anderson, *Hollywood TV: The Studio System in the Fifties* (Austin: University of Texas Press, 1994). I am proud that I worked on the committees for the dissertations that served as the bases for these books by these fine scholars.

NOTES TO CHAPTER 1

1. Sigmund Freud, *Jokes and Their Relation to the Unconscious* (1905), trans. James Strachey (New York: W. W. Norton & Company, 1960), 15.

2. As the preface to this book indicates, this theorization is indebted to conversations with Thomas Schatz in 1991–93.

3. The term is from Paul M. Hirsch, "Processing Fads and Fashions: An Organization-Set Analysis of Cultural Industry Systems," *American Journal of Sociology* 77 (1972): 639–59, rpt. in *Rethinking Popular Culture: Contemporary Perspectives in Cultural Studies,* ed. Chandra Mukerji and Michael Schudson (Berkeley: University of California Press, 1991), 321.

4. Gerard Jones, *Honey, I'm Home!: Sitcoms: Selling the American Dream* (New York: Grove Weidenfeld, 1992), 4.

5. Horace Newcomb, *TV: The Most Popular Art* (Garden City, N.Y.: Anchor Books, 1974), 28–42.

6. Jane Feuer, "The MTM Style," in *MTM: "Quality Television,"* ed. Feuer, Paul Kerr, and Tise Vahimagi (London: British Film Institute, 1984), 35.

7. Abel Green, "Television's Showmanship Test," *Variety,* 13 March 1946, 1.

8. "The New Season Product: Titles, Sources, Themes," *Motion Picture Herald,* 3 June 1939, 15–17.

9. Janet Staiger, "Hybrid or Inbred: The Purity Hypothesis and Hollywood Genre History," *Film Criticism* 22, no. 1 (Fall 1997): 5–20.

10. However, the following is a list of good attempts to define the television situation comedy or provide important critical information: Newcomb, *TV,* 28–58; Jack Gladden, "Archie Bunker Meets Mr. Spoopendyke: Nineteenth-Century Prototypes for Domestic Situation Comedy," *Journal of Popular Culture* 10, no. 1 (Summer 1976): 167–80; Mick Eaton, "Television Situation Comedy," *Screen* 19, no. 4 (Winter 1978/79): 61–89; Arthur Frank Wertheim, *Radio Comedy* (New York: Oxford University Press, 1979)—of particular interest given that television drew formulas and stars directly from radio; John Bryant, "Emma, Lucy and the American Situation Comedy of Manners," *Journal of Popular Culture* 13, no. 2 (Fall 1979): 248–55; Mick Eaton, "Laughter in the Dark," *Screen* 22 no. 2 (1981): 21–28; Barry Curtis, "Aspects of Sitcom," in *Television Sitcom,* ed. Jim Cook, BFI Dossier #17 (London: British Film Institute, 1982), 4–12; Jim Cook, "Narrative, Comedy Character and Performance," in *Television Sitcom,* ed. Cook, 13–18; Terry Lovell, "A Genre of Social Disruption?" in *Television Sitcom,* ed. Cook, 19–31; Mark Crispin Miller, "Prime Time: Deride and Conquer" [1986], rpt. in *Watching Television,* ed. Todd Gitlin (New York: Pantheon Books, 1986), 183–228; Feuer, "MTM Style," 32–60; Susan Horowitz, "Sitcom Domesticus—A Species Endangered by Social Change" [1984], rpt. in *Television: The Critical View,* ed. Horace Newcomb, 4th ed. (New York: Oxford University Press, 1987), 106–11; Patricia Mellencamp, "Situation and Simulation: An Introduction to 'I

Love Lucy,'" *Screen* 26, no. 2 (March–April 1985): 30–40; Nina C. Leibman, "Leave Mother Out: The Fifties Family in American Film and Television," *Wide Angle* 10, no. 4 (1988): 24–41; Robert Deming, "Kate and Allie: 'New Women' and the Audiences' Television Archive," *camera obscura* 16 (January 1988): 154–76; Mary Beth Haralovich, "Sit-Coms and Suburbs: Positioning the 1950s Homemaker" [1988], in *Private Screenings: Television and the Female Consumer,* ed. Lynn Spigel and Denise Mann (Minneapolis: University of Minnesota Press, 1992), 110–41; Nina C. Leibman, *Living Room Lectures: The Fifties Family in Film and Television* (Austin: University of Texas Press, 1995).

11. An outstanding survey of the literature on comedy, humor, and joking is in the introductions to the various sections of Henry Jenkins and Kristine Brunovska Karnick, eds. *Classical Hollywood Comedy* (New York: Routledge, 1995).

12. The problems with using A. C. Nielsen figures are manifold; however, they are the best quantitative data available because of their continuity and explicit description of methodology. Discussions of the history and shortcomings of the Nielsens and its predecessors are in Christopher H. Sterling and John M. Kittross, *Stay Tuned: A Concise History of American Broadcasting* (Belmont, Cal.: Wadsworth Publishing Company, 1978), 126; Hugh Malcolm Beville, Jr., *Audience Ratings: Radio, Television, and Cable,* rev. ed. (Hillsdale, N.J.: Lawrence Erlbaum Associates, 1988); David Boltrack, "The 'Big 3' Networks," *Gannett Center Journal* 2, no. 3 (Summer 1988): 53–62; John Dimling, "A. C. Nielsen: The 'Gold Standard,'" *Gannett Center Journal* 2, no. 3 (Summer 1988): 63–69; Eileen R. Meehan, "Why We Don't Count: The Commodity Audience," in *Logics of Television: Essays in Cultural Criticism,* ed. Patricia Mellencamp (London: British Film Institute, 1990), 117–37; Ien Ang, *Desperately Seeking the Audience* (London: Routledge, 1991); Leibman, *Living Room Lectures,* 84–86. None of these sources do more than also observe the problem that the Nielsens tell us nothing about what an audience is actually doing while the television set is on. Solutions to that problem have included new proposed methods of observation of the living rooms, including using electronic eyes.

Frustrated with what they consider to be undercounting by the Nielsens (as network audiences are declining as a consequence of cable), SRI has offered a commercial alternative. As this work is being written, three networks announced they were funding SRI and might switch to using its information instead of the Nielsens.

Additionally, during the history of the Nielsens, its methods of sampling and categories have changed. Thus, the ratings figures provided below and in subsequent chapters should not be presumed to be equivalent across years without checking on the status of the Nielsens' methods for the time periods being compared. I am assuming that the data for an individual year can be compared across programs for that year. That comparison, however, must be tempered by the overall difficulties with the Nielsens and any quantitative data gathered on audiences.

I have chosen to use ratings rather than shares as my yardstick. A. C. Nielsen defines the terms as follows: ratings are based on the "percent of U.S. TV households tuned to the program"; shares are the "percent of households using television at the time of the program's principal telecast" that are tuned to the programs. Shares help researchers "compare programs telecast at times when TV usage levels are different"; ratings help them see the size of the total audience. From a broadcaster's point of view, both numbers are useful. The rating may be low, but if the share is high, then the program is doing well in competition with what is on the other channels. I am interested in the large-audience question, so ratings are my primary tool, although I will discuss a program's share when it becomes significant to the network's decision-making process.

13. In 1954 only 56 percent of U.S. houses had television sets. By 1959, the number is estimated at 86 percent. Sterling and Kittross, *Stay Tuned,* 535.

14. Longevity is a different problem. Programs may reach a large audience for many years. Examples include *Gunsmoke, Bonanza,* and *Murder, She Wrote.* What produces an apparently faithful audience that is large enough to justify retention of the program requires individual analysis as well. Likely the particular dynamics at each network at the time help account for the phenomenon.

15. Decay for these programs cannot be correlated to their rapid or slower climb to success. *The Beverly Hillbillies* had a rapid move to first place, dropped out of the top ten in its third year, and returned to that level of success for the next four years, giving it seven strong years. Also a fast starter, *Laverne & Shirley* lasted four years in the top ten. Slower-building *All in the Family* and *The Cosby Show* both reached number one within one year, and each made the top ten for seven years, just like *The Beverly Hillbillies*. The slowest of the group, *Happy Days*, took two years to reach top ten status and lasted as long as *Laverne & Shirley*—four years.

16. David Marc, *Demographic Vistas: Television in American Culture* (Philadelphia: University of Pennsylvania Press, 1984), 11.

17. Here begins the traditional review of the literature. In order to accommodate scholars but not bore other readers, I am limiting this survey to discussions of the situation comedy genre and appeals to mass audiences. Not covered is the literature on other popular genres (e.g., discussions of the western or melodrama). I have also not covered here the literature on other hit programs or all television theory.

18. For example, Newcomb suggests the natural aesthetic of television is "intimacy, continuity, and history"; see *TV*, 245. Another strong contender for media specificity is "liveness." From a slightly different angle, some people theorize ontologies for the viewer in relation to the practices of network TV: this is where the notion enters that the sitcom is successful because it fits the short length of the viewers' attention spans.

19. Curtis, "Aspects of Sitcom," 11.

20. Marc, *Demographic Vistas*, 7, quoting Gilbert Seldes, *The Public Arts*.

21. Lauren Rabinovitz, "Sitcoms and Single Moms: Representations of Feminism on American TV," *Cinema Journal* 29, no. 1 (Fall 1989): 5.

22. Also see Leibman, *Living Room Lectures*, who locates a melodramatic underpinning to the domestic sitcoms of the 1950s and early 1960s.

23. Curtis, "Aspects of Sitcom," 11.

24. John Fiske, *Television Culture* (London: Methuen, 1987), 45.

25. Darrell Y. Hamamoto, *Nervous Laughter: Television Situation Comedy and Liberal Democratic Ideology* (New York: Praeger, 1989), 1.

26. Rabinovitz, "Sitcoms and Single Moms," 3.

27. Todd Gitlin, *Inside Prime Time* (New York: Pantheon Books, 1983), 215.

28. Other examples of this are Horowitz, "Sitcom Domesticus," 106–11, and Paul Kerr, "The Making of (The) MTM (Show)," in *MTM: "Quality Television,"* ed. Feuer, Kerr, and Vahimagi, 61.

29. For brief and excellent reviews of these theories, see the editors' introductions in Jenkins and Karnick, *Classical Hollywood Comedy,* and Chris Powell and George E. C. Paton, Introduction, in *Humor in Society: Resistance and Control,* ed. Powell and Paton (London: Macmillan, 1988), xiii–xxi.

30. Curtis, "Aspects of Sitcom," 9. Newcomb also provides an earlier, less developed version of this in *TV,* 262.

31. Fiske, *Television Culture,* 239.

32. Miller, "Prime Time," 194. Richard Butsch also sees the U.S. network sitcom as anti-dads, although he limits the attack to working-class fathers. "Class and Gender in Four Decades of Television Situation Comedy: Plus Ça Change," *Critical Studies in Mass Communication* 9 (December 1992): 387–99.

33. Mellencamp, "Situation and Simulation," 32.

34. Mimi White, "What's the Difference: *Frank's Place* in Television," *Wide Angle* 13, nos. 3/4 (1991): 84.

35. As Justin Wyatt has reminded me, the issue of whether the audiences for programs are duplicated or not is important to advertisers who desire to plan product campaigns on the basis of reach into the potential audience.

36. Marc, *Demographic Vistas,* 5. For a survey and counterargument, see Janet Staiger, *Interpreting Films: Studies in the Historical Reception of American Cinema* (Princeton, N.J.: Princeton University Press, 1992).

37. Gitlin, *Inside Prime Time,* 217–18. Also see Feuer, "MTM Style," 56–58, and Fiske, *Television Culture,* 19.

38. Fiske, *Television Culture,* 77.

39. Mary Ann Watson, "[From *My Little Margie* to *Murphy Brown*:] Images of Women [on Television]," *Television Quarterly* 27, no. 2 (1994): 4–24.

NOTES TO CHAPTER 2

1. John P. Shanley, "TV: Simplicity Rescues One of Four Weekly Comedies," *New York Times,* 1 October 1962, 63.

2. "Rose," "*Beverly Hillbillies,*" *Variety,* 3 October 1962, n.p.

3. "The New Season," *Time,* 12 October 1962, 97–9; "The New Season," *Newsweek,* 15 October 1962, 96–97.

4. Jack Gould, "TV: 'Beverly Hillbillys' [*sic*]," *New York Times,* 2 November 1962, 63.

5. "On the Cob," *Time,* 30 November 1962, 76.

6. "The Corn Is Green," *Newsweek,* 3 December 1962, 70.

7. These journals and the *Saturday Evening Post* (mentioned below) have variable abilities to reach members of the viewing public; however, two of them are very large, mass circulation periodicals. The circulation of *TV Guide* in 1962 was over 8,000,000; *Saturday Review* reached only about 300,000; the *Saturday Evening Post*'s published circulation was over 6,600,000.

8. Gilbert Seldes, "The Beverly Hillbillies," *TV Guide,* 15 December 1962, 4.

9. Robert Lewis Shayon, "Innocent Jeremiah," *Saturday Review,* 5 January 1963, 32.

10. Richard Warren Lewis, "The Golden Hillbillies," *Saturday Evening Post,* 2 February 1963, 30+.

11. I have tried to walk a fine line here, avoiding any clear claims about what caused the blockbuster success. The comedy of the program was one very strong factor. An initially strong publicity machine helped bring in early viewers, but it could not have held the audience if the program had been unattractive. It is the case that the numbers do increase

as the cultural reinterpretation occurs. One explanation is that people who enjoyed highbrow reading strategies were now able to watch it. However, without any further breakdowns in the Nielsens, I cannot argue this. See below.

12. Roland Marchand, "Visions of Classlessness, Quests for Dominion: American Popular Culture, 1945–60," in *Reshaping America: Society and Institutions, 1945–1960,* ed. Robert H. Bremner and Gary W. Reichard (Columbus: Ohio State University Press, 1982), 166.

13. Norman Jacobs, Introduction, *Culture for the Millions? Mass Media in Modern Society* (Boston: Beacon Press, 1959), xii. The papers are previously published in *Daedalus* 89, no. 2 (Spring 1960).

14. Theodor W. Adorno and Max Horkheimer, "The Culture Industry: Enlightenment as Mass Deception" [1944], in *Dialectic of Enlightenment,* trans. John Cumming (New York: Herder and Herder, 1972), 137.

15. Leo Rosten, "The Intellectual and the Mass Media: Some Rigorously Random Remarks," in *Culture for the Millions?* ed. Jacobs, 71.

16. Andrew Ross, *No Respect: Intellectuals and Popular Culture* (New York: Routledge, 1989), 42–54. Also see Lynn Spigel, "From Domestic Space to Outer Space: The 1960s Fantastic Family Sit-Com," in *Close Encounters: Film, Feminism, and Science Fiction,* ed. Constance Penley, Elisabeth Lyon, Lynn Spigel, and Janet Bergstrom (Minneapolis: University of Minnesota Press, 1991), 206–12.

17. Arthur Schlesinger, Jr., "Notes on a National Cultural Policy," in *Culture for the Millions?* ed. Jacobs, 148–54.

18. Michael Curtin, *Redeeming the Wasteland: Television Documentary and Cold War Politics* (New Brunswick, N.J.: Rutgers University Press, 1995), 27.

19. Newton N. Minow, *Equal Time: The Private Broadcaster and the Public Interest* (New York: Athenaeum, 1964), 4.

20. Erik Barnouw, *Tube of Plenty: The Evolution of American Television,* rev. ed. (Oxford: Oxford University Press, 1982), 299–306.

21. Minow wasn't the only aggressor toward industry practices at this time. During 1961–62, Senate hearings on televised crime and vio-

lence and juvenile delinquency were also instrumental in restraining explicit representations.

22. Lawrence Bergreen, *Look Now, Pay Later: The Rise of Network Broadcasting* (New York: Doubleday and Co., 1980), 212–23; William Boddy, "Building the World's Largest Advertising Medium: CBS and Television, 1940–60," in *Hollywood in the Age of Television*, ed. Tino Balio (Boston: Unwin Hyman, 1990), 82–83; Barnouw, *Tube of Plenty*, 260–65; Robert Metz, *CBS: Reflections in a Bloodshot Eye* (New York: Playboy Press, 1975), 216–41. John Caldwell notes that 1950s television habitually represented high art ambivalently, arguing that its address was certainly to the working class; see *Televisuality: Style, Crisis, and Authority in American Television* (New Brunswick, N.J.: Rutgers University Press, 1995), 32–35.

23. Minow, *Equal Time*, 67.

24. Robert Lewis Shayon, "Do the People Care," *Saturday Review*, 27 May 1961, 25.

25. Another fallout of the Minow speech was further questioning of about what the people did care. See Gary A. Steiner, *The People Look at Television: A Study of Audience Attitudes* (New York: Alfred A. Knopf, 1963).

26. "Television: 1961–62 Season," *Changing Times* 15, no. 9 (September 1961): 5. Also see direct references to this program as rebuking Minow in Gould, "TV: Beverly Hillbillys [*sic*]," 63; Lewis, "Golden Hillbillies," 30 [opening paragraph].

27. Fred J. MacDonald, *One Nation under Television: The Rise and Decline of Network TV* (Chicago: Nelson-Hall Publishers, 1994), 149.

28. A. C. Nielsen Company, *National Nielsen TV Ratings* (A. C. Nielsen 1962). For the first year of *The Beverly Hillbillies*, I was able to view data for the weeks of 9 September 1962 through 23 December 1962. On the Nielsens' shift in 1963 to eleven sets of demographic breaks, see Nina Leibman, *Living Room Lectures: The Fifties Family in Film and Television* (Austin: University of Texas Press, 1995), 84–86.

29. Stephen Cox reports that Irene Ryan's agent believed that African Americas were particularly fond of Ryan; Max Baer thought

that Southerners, blacks, and poor people were program devotees. This is merely speculation, however. *The Beverly Hillbillies* (New York: HarperCollins Publishers, 1993), 155–56.

30. David Marc, *Comic Visions: Television Comedy and American Culture* (Boston: Unwin Hyman, 1989), 128.

31. David Marc, *Demographic Vistas: Television in American Culture* (Philadelphia: University of Pennsylvania Press, 1984), 55.

32. Donna McCrohan, *Prime Time, Our Time: America's Life and Times through the Prism of Television* (Rocklin, Cal.: Prima Publishing & Communications, 1990), 128.

33. Paul Attallah, *Situation Comedy and "The Beverly Hillbillies": The Unworthy Discourse* (Montreal, Quebec: Working Papers in Communication, McGill University, 1983), 26–30.

34. McCrohan, *Prime Time*, 131.

35. CBS News Press Release, 16 July 1962, in Academy of Motion Picture Arts and Sciences clipping file for "Buddy Ebsen."

36. "J.H.," "Hillbillies Laughing It Up," *New York Herald Tribune,* 4 November 1962, n.p. in New York Public Library Lincoln Center clipping file for *Beverly Hillbillies.*

37. Shayon, "Innocent Jeremiah," 32.

38. Arnold Hano, "The G.A.P. Loves the 'Hillbillies,'" *New York Times Magazine,* 17 November 1963, 30.

39. Lawrence Laurent, "'Hillbillies' Merits Award but from Whom, for What?" *Los Angeles Times,* 10 June 1963, sec. 4, p. 17.

40. As noted in chapter 1, my method of analysis and sampling of the series will depend on the discourse around the program. Here the interest is in amplifying the public commentary through textual analysis of the plots and types of humor used during the first year of the program. The four programs watched were "The Clampetts Strike Oil" (episode no. 1, air date 26 September 1962), "Getting Settled" (no. 2, 3 October 1962), "Jed Buys a Freeway" (no. 23, 27 February 1963), and "Jed Becomes a Banker" (no. 24, 6 March 1963). The choices were based on easy availability through commercial rereleases of episodes. Sampling of episodes from the beginning of the second season suggests

that the show did not change to any significant degree as a result of the public discourse. Its satire or surface "fun" remained focused on verbal and visual humor, with no vitriolic attacks on pretentious people. Observed were: "Granny Gets a Garden" (no. 39), "Elly Starts to School" (no. 40), and "The Clampett Look" (no. 41), air dates in September and October 1963. Titles and episode numbers are from Joel Eisner and David Krinsky, *Television Comedy Series: An Episode Guide to 153 TV Sitcoms in Syndication* (Jefferson, N.C.: McFarland & Company, 1984). Air dates are from the local area *TV Guide* on microfilm at the University of Texas at Austin general libraries.

41. *The Beverly Hillbillies* also fits the trend noted by Spigel that at the start of the 1960s, domestic comedies were structured around families in which single parenting was common. See Spigel, "From Domestic Space to Outer Space."

42. Attallah, *Situation Comedy*, 27–28.

43. MacDonald, *One Nation under Television*, 170.

44. Chris J. Magoc argues that in the late 1960s, comedies such as *Green Acres, Lassie,* and *The Beverly Hillbillies* did address social issues—specifically, environment concerns. The programs, however, did not raise controversial claims or offer radical solutions. "The Machine in the Wasteland: Progress, Pollution, and the Pastoral in Rural-Based Television, 1954–1971," *Journal of Popular Film and Television* 19, no. 1 (Spring 1991):25. Spigel discusses late 1960s discussions of the space program; Spigel, "From Domestic Space to Outer Space."

NOTES TO CHAPTER 3

1. Dorothy Rabinowitz, "Watching the Sit-Coms," *Commentary* 60, no. 4 (October 1975): 70.

2. Todd Gitlin, *Inside Prime Time* (New York: Pantheon Books, 1983), 212–13; Vince Waldron, *Classic Sitcoms: A Celebration of the Best Prime-Time Comedy* (New York: Macmillan, 1987), 185–86. Waldron indicates the two concessions were eliminating a "goddamn it" in

Archie's dialogue and deleting a shot of Mike zipping up his pants as he came downstairs.

3. "CBS Bigot Sitcom Fails to Light Up Switchboard; Pros Outnumber Cons, but Show Preems Soft in Overnights," *Variety,* 20 January 1971, n.p.; "CBS Bigot's Double Exposure," *Variety,* 13 January 1971, n.p.

4. "CBS Bigot Sitcom Fails to Light Up Switchboard," n.p.

5. *TV Guide* [Austin, Texas, area edition], 12 January 1971, A-43.

6. "CBS Bigot Sitcom Fails to Light Up Switchboard," n.p.

7. Donna McCrohan, *Archie and Edith, Mike and Gloria: The Tumultuous History of "All in the Family"* (New York: Workman Publishing, 1987), 25.

8. McCrohan, *Archie and Edith,* 25–26.

9. Richard Burgheim, "The New Season: Perspiring with Relevance," *Time,* 28 September 1970, 66.

10. McCrohan, *Archie and Edith,* 27–28.

11. Dwight Newton, "Introduction to a Bigot," *San Francisco Examiner,* 12 January 1971, rpt. in *All in the Family: A Critical Appraisal,* ed. Richard P. Adler (New York: Praeger, 1979), 81–82.

12. "Bill," *"All in the Family," Variety,* 13 January 1971, n.p.

13. Cecil Smith, "Bigotry Used as a Laughing Matter," *Los Angles Times,* 12 January 1971, part 4, p. 4; Alan Bunce, "'All in the Family': TV Social Departure," *Christian Science Monitor,* 18 January 1971, rpt. in *All in the Family,* ed. Adler, 82.

14. H. B. Crowther, Jr., "The Stuff of Dreams," *Newsweek,* 18 January 1971, 55.

15. Pamela Haynes, "New TV Comedy Takes Hard, Realistic Poke at Bigotry," *Los Angeles Sentinel,* 28 January 1971, in *All in the Family,* ed. Adler, 84–85. *The Doris Day Show* did rank number ten in the ratings for 1969–70.

16. Whitney M. Young, Jr., "Irresponsible Television Production Aids Racism," *Los Angeles Sentinel,* 4 February 1971, rpt. in *All in the Family,* ed. Adler, 85–86; Fred Ferretti, "TV: Are Racism and Bigotry Funny," *New York Times,* 12 January 1971, 70; Stephanie Harrington,

"The Message Sounds Like 'Hate Thy Neighbor,'" *New York Times,* 24 January 1971, sec. 2, p. 17.

17. "Tone," "Telepic Review: *All in the Family,*" *Daily Variety* (Hollywood), 13 January 1971, rpt. in *All in the Family,* ed. Adler, 70; Harrington, "The Message Sounds Like 'Hate Thy Neighbor,'" sec. 2, p. 17. Also see Richard Burgheim, "Recycled Waste," *Time,* 1 February 1971, 64. *All in the Family* had returned to the live practices of 1950s television, using a stage proscenium and taping multicamera before a studio audience. This significantly differentiated the series from its contemporary competitors. "Bill" in *Variety* noted that as an asset, but then "Bill" was a proponent of the show. "Bill," "All in the Family," n.p.

18. Smith, "Bigotry Used as a Laughing Matter," p. 12.

19. Smith, "Bigotry Used as a Laughing Matter," p. 12.

20. Ernie Kreiling, "A Closer Look at Television," *Valley News,* 5 February 1971, 2-B, in University of Southern California clipping file for *All in the Family.*

21. Newton, "Introduction to a Bigot," 81; Clarence Petersen, "CBS Debuts Courageous New Comedy," *New York Daily Mirror,* 15 January 1971, 23.

22. Ratings for period ending 6 February 1971, A. C. Nielsen Company, *National Nielsen TV Ratings* (A. C. Nielsen, 1971) [hereafter Nielsens].

23. Ratings for period ending 20 February 1971, Nielsens.

24. Ratings for period ending 1 March 1971, Nielsens.

25. "Bill," "All in the Family," n.p.; Petersen, "CBS Debuts Courageous New Comedy," 23. O'Connor's previous acting roles would not feed into this response. Of the some twenty-six films he worked in from 1960, his more famous roles were as a gangster in *Point Blank* (1967) and a general in *What Did You Do in the War Daddy?* (1966). That latter role is sometimes described as catching Lear and Yorkin's eye, leading to the hiring of O'Connor as Archie.

26. Mary Lois Vann, "*All in the Family,*" *Women's Wear Daily,* 12 January 1971, n.p.; Newton, "Introduction to a Bigot," 81; Ferretti,

"TV: Are Racism and Bigotry Funny?" 70; "Bill," "*All in the Family,*" n.p.; Bunce, "'All in the Family': TV Social Departure," 83.

27. Although the description of *All in the Family* for the premiere episode locates the Bunkers as "middle class," critics variably refer as well to their status as being "lower middle class" or "working class." I personally associate highly with the representations in the program and recall that I knew I could always get a rise from my father by declaring we were a working-class family; dad insisted we were middle class. This issue was one of pride that he was raising our socioeconomic status. That slippage among class designations has easy explanations from sociological, linguistic, and economic theory, and its existence among the responses is symptomatic of not only the historical period but larger trends in American social and economic life.

28. Ironically, Robert Wood had only just not renewed Jackie Gleason's most recent show as part of his attempt to shift the CBS lineup.

29. Robert Lewis Shayon, "Love That Hate," *Saturday Review* 54 (27 March 1971): 20.

30. Norman Mark, "'All in the Family' Gets Better As Weeks Go By," *Chicago Daily News,* 23 February 1971, rpt. in *All in the Family,* ed. Adler, 87–88.

31. Jack Gould, "Can Bigotry Be Laughed Away? It's Worth a Try," *New York Times,* 21 February 1971, sec. 2, p. 15; John Leonard, "Bigotry as a Dirty Joke," *Life* 70 (19 March 1971): 10.

32. Gould, "Can Bigotry Be Laughed Away?" p. 15; Tom Mackin, "Bigot Is Star of TV Series," *Newark Evening News,* 28 February, 1971, E1; "Family Fun," *Newsweek* 77 (15 March 1971): 64 and 68; Shayon, "Love That Hate," 20.

33. Ratings for period ending 17 April 1971, Nielsens.

34. Cleveland Amory, "*All in the Family,*" *TV Guide,* 27 February 1971, 18, rpt. in *All in the Family,* ed. Adler, 89.

35. Donna McCrohan, *Prime Time, Our Time: America's Life and Times Through the Prism of Television* (Rocklin, CAL.: Prima Publishing & Communications, 1990), 210.

36. Robert Wood quoted in Paul Kerr, "The Making of (the) MTM

(Show)," in *MTM: "Quality Television,"* ed. Jane Feuer, Paul Kerr and Tise Vahimagi (London: British Film Institute, 1984), 65. Also see pp. 63–67.

37. "History of Television," *TV Guide Almanac,* ed. Craig T. Norback and Peter G. Norback (New York: Ballantine Books, 1980), 392.

38. Les Brown, *Televi$ion: The Business behind the Box* (New York: Harcourt Brace Jovanovich, 1971), 78–98.

39. Brown, *Televi$ion,* 47–58.

40. Sally Bedell, *Up the Tube: Prime-Time TV and the Silverman Years* (New York: Viking, 1981), 9–10; Lawrence Bergreen, *Look Now, Pay Later: The Rise of Network Broadcasting* (New York: Doubleday and Co., 1980), 224–34.

41. "History of Television," 395; "The Losers are . . . ," *Time* 97 (29 March 1971): 50 and 52.

42. "NBC Leads Web in Nominations for Emmys with Nearly Half the 208," *Variety,* 14 April 1971, 32; John J. O'Connor, "TV: See Any Good Sitcoms Lately?" *New York Times,* 21 April 1971, 95. The *New York Times* reports that *All in the Family's* ranking moved from the 50s through March to 14th in mid-April. Whether this occurred before or after the Emmy nominations isn't clear. "'All in the Family' Takes First Place in Nielsen Ratings," *New York Times,* 25 May 1971, 79.

43. "History of Television," 392–95.

44. Bedell, *Up the Tube,* 54.

45. "History of Television," 389 and 395.

46. The fact that Jean Stapleton won the Emmy for Outstanding Actress in a Comedy Series might be suggestive as to causes for the interest of women in the program.

47. Ratings for period ending 22 May 1971, Nielsens; ratings for period ending 9 October 1971, Nielsens.

48. McCohan, *Archie and Edith,* 36; Timothy P. Meyer, "The Impact of 'All in the Family' on Children," *Journal of Broadcasting* 20 (Winter 1976), rpt. in *All in the Family,* ed. Adler, 159. The appeal of the program to women and children can be explained in various ways. Part might be the debunking, if you will, of the father. Moreover, as the show

progressed, episodes featuring issues affecting Gloria and Edith took center stage. Finally, as with *Beavis and Butthead* or *South Park,* the breaking of social taboos likely thrilled children.

49. "NBC-TV Tops in Emmys with 33; 'Moore,' PBS, 'Senator' Hit It Big," *Variety,* 12 May 1971, 208. *All in the Family* received Emmys for Outstanding Comedy Series, Outstanding New Series, and Continued Performance in Comedy Series—Actress (Jean Stapleton). *The Mary Tyler Moore Show* took four: Comedy Supporting Actor (Edward Asner), Comedy Supporting Actress (Valerie Harper), Comedy Series Director (Jay Sandrich), and Comedy Series Writer (James L. Brooks and Allan Burns). In 1971–72, *All in the Family* took home six Emmys including ones for O'Connor, Stapleton, Sally Struthers, director John Rich, and writer Burt Styler. "Stifle yourself, you dingbats!" ad, *Variety,* 19 May 1971, 49.

50. "'All in the Family' Takes First Place in Nielsen Ratings," *New York Times,* 25 May 1971, 79.

51. For fall 1971, the lineup was *All in the Family, Funny Face, The New Dick Van Dyke Show,* and *The Mary Tyler Moore Show.* For fall 1972: *All in the Family, Bridget Loves Bernie, Mary Tyler Moore, The Bob Newhart Show.* For fall 1973: *All in the Family, M*A*S*H, Mary Tyler Moore, Bob Newhart.* For fall 1974: *All in the Family,* Paul Sand in *Friends and Lovers, Mary Tyler Moore, Bob Newhart.* For fall 1975, CBS broke this setup but attempted to maintain its ratings' hold with a similar sitcom lineup: *The Jeffersons* (a spin-off of *All in the Family*), *Doc, Mary Tyler Moore,* and *Bob Newhart.*

52. Ratings for period ending 18 December 1971, Nielsens.

53. Laura Z. Hobson, "As I Listened to Archie Say 'Hebe' . . . ," *New York Times,* 12 September 1971, sec. 2, p. 27.

54. Norman Lear, "As I Read How Laura Saw Archie . . . ," *New York Times,* 10 October 1971, rpt. in *All in the Family,* ed. Adler, 110.

55. Significant instances in this debate are John J. O'Connor, "TV Review," *New York Times,* 20 September 1971, 53; "Archie: Lovable or Lamentable?" [letters to the editor], *New York Times,* 3 October 1971, sec. 2, pp. 17–18, 36; Nat Hentoff, "You Know You're Going . . . ," *Vil-*

lage Voice, 14 October 1971, n.p., in New York Public Library Lincoln Center [hereafter NYPL-LC] clipping file for *All in the Family;* Howard Kissel, "All in the Family," *Women's Wear Daily,* 20 October 1971, n.p., in NYPL-LC clipping file for *All in the Family;* Peggy Hudson, "'Kids Are Fed Up with Baloney,'" *Senior Scholastic 99,* no. 6 (25 October 1971): 6–7, 22; Leonard Gross, "Big, Bigger, Bigot," *Los Angeles Times West Magazine,* 21 November 1971, 19+; "TV: Speaking about the Unspeakable," *Newsweek* 78, no. 22 (29 November 1971): 52–60. Throughout the fall, interviews, articles, and other materials continued to be churned out about the program, including several interesting interviews with families whose lives might be said to resemble those of the Bunkers; see Marshall Frady, "It's All in This Family, Too," *Life* 71, no. 21 (19 November 1971): 61+. That many of the articles in the Hobson discussion were in New York City papers might account for the strong showing New York gave to the program by the end of the fall. A valuable later essay not part of the Hobson series is Charles L. Sanders, "Is Archie Bunker the Real White America?" *Ebony* 27, no. 8 (June 1972): 186–88+.

56. Arnold Hano, "Can Archie Bunker Give Bigotry a Bad Name?" *New York Times Magazine,* 12 March 1972, 33.

57. Myron Roberts and Lincoln Haynes, "TV: Archie's Hang-Ups," *Nation* 213, no. 16 (15 November 1971): 509.

58. In the pilot, Edith Bunker calls President Richard Nixon "tricky Dicky," to the delight of many reviewers. Noting which events in the programs writers tended to describe in their reviews would be a valuable exercise in studying more specific details of the reception of the program. What struck the writers as novel or amusing could illuminate cultural norms.

59. John Slawson, "How Funny Can Bigotry Be?" *Educational Broadcasting Review* (April 1972), rpt. in *All in the Family,* ed. Adler, 115 and 120.

60. Neil Vidmar and Milton Rokeach, "Archie Bunker's Bigotry: A Study in Selective Perception and Exposure," *Journal of Communication* 24, no. 2 (Winter 1974): 36–47; also see Stuart H. Surlin, "Bigotry

on the Air and in Life: The Archie Bunker Case," *Public Telecommunications Review* 2, no. 2 (April 1974): 34–41; John C. Brigham and Linda W. Griesbrecht, "'All in the Family': Racial Attitudes," *Journal of Communication* (Autumn 1976), rpt. in *All in the Family*, ed. Adler, 139–46 (revises and refutes part of Vidman and Rokeach study); G. Cleveland Wilhoit and Harold de Bock, "*All in the Family* in Holland," *Journal of Communication* (Autumn 1976), rpt. in *All in the Family*, ed. Adler, 146–58 (refutes part of Vidmar and Rokeach); John D. Leckenby and Stuart H. Surlin, "Incidental Social Learning and Viewer Race: 'All in the Family' and 'Sanford and Son,'" *Journal of Broadcasting* 20, no. 4 (Fall 1976): 481–94; Meyer, "Impact of 'All in the Family' on Children," 159–69 (impact depends on age); David William Mills, "*All in the Family* and Adolescents: A Study in Perception" (MA thesis, University of Texas at Austin, 1979).

61. Early humanist scholarship is in Howard F. Stein, "*All in the Family* as a Mirror of Contemporary American Culture," *Family Process* 13, no. 3 (September 1974): 279–315; Horace Newcomb, *TV: The Most Popular Art* (Garden City, N.Y.: Anchor Books, 1974), 218; Dennis E. Showalter, "Archie Bunker, Lenny Bruce, and Ben Cartwright: Taboo-Breaking and Character Identification in 'All in the Family,'" *Journal of Popular Culture* 9, no. 3 (Winter 1975): 618–21; Jack Gladden, "Archie Bunker meets Mr. Spoopendyke: Nineteenth-Century Prototypes for Domestic Situation Comedy," *Journal of Popular Culture* 10, no. 1 (Summer 1976): 167–80.

NOTES TO CHAPTER 4

1. Michael Wolff, "What Do You Do at Midnight? You See a Trashy Movie," *New York Times,* 7 September 1975, sec. 2, p. 17.

2. "*Happy Days,*" *Variety,* 17 September 1975, n.p.

3. "Bok," "*Happy Days,*" *Variety,* 23 January 1974, n.p.

4. "Network Rating Scoreboard," *Variety,* 14 April 1976, 57.

5. Alan L. Gansberg, "The 'Happy Days' Story," *Hollywood Reporter 1983–84 TV Preview,* H5, in University of Southern California

[hereafter USC] clipping file for *Happy Days;* Garry Marshall, *Wake Me When It's Funny: How to Break into Show Business and Stay There* (Holbrook, Mass.: Adams Publishing, 1995), 91–93.

6. This was likely also facilitated by the concurrent Broadway success of *Grease,* another retrospective look at the 1950s.

7. This chapter is not the place to develop a theory of nostalgia, but valuable discussions about "nostalgia" in the late 1970s and American film culture are in James Monaco, *American Film Now: The People, the Power, the Money, the Movies* (New York: New American Library, 1979), 60; Fredric Jameson, "On Magic Realism in Film," *Critical Inquiry* 12, no. 2 (Winter 1986): 309; John G. Cawelti, "*Chinatown* and Generic Transformation in Recent American Films" [1979], in *Film Theory and Criticism,* ed. Gerald Mast and Marshall Cohen, 3d ed. (New York: Oxford University Press, 1985), 513. Most writers consider nostalgia to be some kind of pathology: Jameson writes of it as a substitution or displacement by a pseudo-past; Theodor Adorno considers it a refusal to restore a damaged collective narcissism; Anton Kaes finds it to be fantasy work. See Miriam Hansen, "Dossier on *Heimat,*" *New German Critique,* no. 36 (Fall 1985): 4–5; Anton Kaes, *From Hitler to Heimat: The Return of History as Film* (Cambridge: Harvard University Press, 1989), 14–15.

8. "Mosk," "*American Graffiti,*" *Variety,* 20 June 1973, n.p.; Stephen Farber, "'Graffiti' Ranks with 'Bonnie and Clyde,'" *New York Times,* 5 August 1973, sec. 2, p. 4; Roger Greenspun, "*American Graffiti,*" *New York Times,* 13 August 1973, 21; Jay Cocks, "Fabulous '50s," *Time* 102 (20 August 1973): 58; Stanley Kauffmann, "*American Graffiti,*" *New Republic,* 15 September 1973, 22 and 33; Vincent Canby, "'Heavy Traffic' and 'American Graffiti'—Two of the Best," *New York Times,* 16 September 1973, sec. 2, p. 1; Aljean Harmetz [a woman], "Our Own Past Is in 'Graffiti,'" *New York Times,* 2 December 1973, sec. 2, p. 13.

9. "Mosk," "*American Graffiti,*" n.p.

10. Farber, "'Graffiti' Ranks with 'Bonnie and Clyde,'" p. 4.

11. Harmetz, "Our Own Past Is in 'Graffiti,'" p. 13.

12. "Tone," "*Happy Days,*" *Daily Variety,* 15 January 1974, n.p., in USC clipping file for *Happy Days;* "Bok," "*Happy Days,*" *Variety,* 23 January 1974, n.p.; Cleveland Amory, "*Happy Days,*" *TV Guide,* 30 March 1974, 28. Also see M. T. Paige, "TV," *Los Angeles Voice,* 15 February 1974, n.p., in USC clipping file for *Happy Days.*

13. "Bok," "*Happy Days,*" n.p.

14. Ratings for the period ending 9 February 1974, A. C. Nielsen Company, *National Nielsen TV Ratings* (A. C. Nielsen) [hereafter Nielsens]; ratings for the period beginning 19 December 1971, Nielsens.

15. Benjamin Stein, "When Growing Up Was Not Absurd," *Wall Street Journal,* 26 March 1974, n.p., in USC clipping file for *Happy Days.*

16. Stein, "When Growing Up Was Not Absurd," n.p.; Gansberg, "'Happy Days' Story," H6.

17. Donna McCrohan, *Prime Time, Our Time: America's Life and Times through the Prism of Television* (Rocklin, Cal.: Prima Publishing & Communications, 1990), 260.

18. Explanations of this sort for the success of *Happy Days* and *Laverne & Shirley* are in Darrell Y. Hamamoto, *Nervous Laughter: Television Situation Comedy and Liberal Democratic Ideology* (New York: Praeger, 1989), and Ella Taylor, *Prime-Time Families: Television Culture in Postwar America* (Berkeley: University of California Press, 1989). As I shall suggest below, while I don't discount these factors, I also do not think that what made *Laverne & Shirley* number one was primarily connected to American culture specifically as it existed in 1976.

19. Estimated average ratings for spring 1975, Nielsens.

20. McCrohan, *Prime Time,* 219.

21. One consequence of this decision was that *All in the Family* had to move out of its treasured Saturday lead-in spot. It went to Mondays at 9 P.M. with *Rhoda* and *Phyllis* as the lead-ins. Several individuals including Norman Lear, Carroll O'Connor, Alan Alda, and Mary Tyler Moore argued that the family hour violated free speech, and in November 1976 a Los Angeles district judge agreed it was censorship. Still, network broadcasters are fairly sensitive to what they put into the first two

hours of prime time. McCrohan, *Prime Time,* 219; "History of Television," in *TV Guide Almanac,* ed. Craig T. Norback and Peter G. Norback (New York: Ballantine Books, 1980), 401–3.

22. "History of Television," 402–3. An August 1977 Harris survey indicated that 71 percent of the American public thought programs had too much violence, up 12 percent from 1968. In October 1977, Tipper Gore led fifty wives of congressmen to begin a campaign against TV violence.

23. Lawrence Bergreen, *Look Now, Pay Later: The Rise of Network Broadcasting* (New York: Doubleday and Co., 1980), 234. Also see Jane Feuer, "MTM Enterprises: An Overview," in *MTM: "Quality Television,"* ed. Feuer, Paul Kerr and Tise Vahimagi (London: British Film Institute, 1984), 16–17; Gary Deeb, "The Man Who Destroyed Television," *Playboy* 26 (October 1979): 216–20; David J. Londoner, "The Changing Economics of Entertainment" [1978/79], rpt. in *The American Film Industry,* ed. Tino Balio, rev. ed. (Madison: University of Wisconsin Press, 1985), 610; Leslie Fishbein, "*Roots*: Docudrama and the Interpretation of History," in *American History/American Television: Interpreting the Video Past,* ed. John E. O'Connor (New York: Ungar, 1983), 279–80.

24. Gansberg, "'Happy Days' Story," H6.

25. McCrohan, *Prime Time,* 219.

26. Gansberg, "'Happy Days' Story," H6; Marshall, *Wake Me When It's Funny,* 164.

27. "*Happy Days,*" *Variety,* 17 September 1975, n.p.

28. All episodes are directed by Jerry Paris. These examples were picked somewhat randomly. I primarily used personal availability and arbitrary selection.

29. Research by David Bordwell, myself, and Kristin Thompson indicates that an average Hollywood film from the period of 1929 through 1960 had average shot lengths of 10 to 11 seconds, "twice that of the silent decade." The range, however, could be wide, from 3.7 seconds in von Stroheim's *Wedding March* (1928) to 37 seconds in *Caravan* (1934). *The Classical Hollywood Cinema: Film Style and*

Mode of Production to 1960 (London: Routledge and Kegan Paul, 1985), 61.

30. Bob Knight, "TV Ratings Tight, but Not Yet Tipsy," *Variety*, 1 October 1975, 83; "Weekly Rating Scorecard," *Variety*, 8 October 1975, 43; "TV Series Ratings after Seven Weeks," *Variety*, 5 November 1975, 46 (for period ending 26 October 1975); Bob Knight, "Average '75 Ratings Decline: 3 Points," *Variety*, 12 November 1975, 39; "Network Series Rating Averages," *Variety*, 11 February 1976, 52 (average for season up to start of "second season" on 19 January 1976).

31. Co-creator Garry Marshall was continually looking for spin-offs for *Happy Days*, a standard practice in independent and network production. An episode using his sister, Penny Marshall, and Cindy Williams as dates for the *Happy Days* crew seemed to work, and the network agreed to pick up Marshall's proposal for a new program starring Marshall and Williams. The *Happy Days* episode showed during fall 1975, and then the premiere of *Laverne & Shirley* combined both series to maximize audience interest.

32. John J. O'Connor, "TV: 'Laverne and Shirley,' Spin-off with Surprise," *New York Times*, 27 January 1976, 63; "Mor," "*Laverne & Shirley*," *Variety*, 4 February 1970, n.p.; Cleveland Amory, "Laverne and Shirley," *TV Guide*, 20 March 1976, 36; Harry F. Waters, "Blue-Collar Boffo," *Newsweek* 87 (29 March 1976): 85. Also see Robert Sklar, *Prime-Time America: Life on and behind the Television Screen* (New York: Oxford University Press, 1980), 15–18, 22–23, 68–69.

33. Cecil Smith, "ABC Spin-off Debuts Tonight," *Los Angeles Times*, 27 January 1976, part 4, p. 14.

34. Amory, "Laverne and Shirley," 36; Waters, "Blue-Collar Boffo," 85.

35. "'Second Season' Ratings Averages," *Variety*, 17 March 1976, 63; "Network Rating Scorecard," *Variety*, 14 April 1976, 57; "1975–76 Regular Series Ratings," *Variety*, 28 April 1976, 44.

36. "Preem Week's Top 30 Rankings," *Variety*, 26 September 1976, 53; "Weekly Rating Scorecard," *Variety*, 6 October 1976, 41; "ABC Even Takes Series Week as Ratings Dominance Continues," *Variety*, 27

October 1976, 51; "Regular Series' Top 40 after Five Weeks," *Variety*, 3 November 1976, 42.

37. Ratings for period ending 1 January 1977, Nielsens; ratings for fall 1976, Nielsens.

38. "*Laverne & Shirley*," *Variety*, 6 September 1978, n.p. Also see Burt Perlutsky, "It May Be Called 'Laverne & Shirley' . . . ," *TV Guide*, 22 May 1976, 21–24; Morna Murphy, "Laverne and Shirley: 'Drive!' She Said," *Hollywood Reporter*, 28 September 1976, n.p., in USC clipping file for *Laverne & Shirley*; "Whit," "*Laverne & Shirley*," *Variety*, 22 September 1977, n.p., in USC clipping file for *Laverne & Shirley*. Academics included McCrohan, *Prime Time*, 263; Lynn C. Spangler, "A Historical Overview of Female Friendships on Prime-Time Television," *Journal of Popular Culture* 22, no. 4 (Spring 1989): 18; and Alexander Doty, *Making Things Perfectly Queer: Interpreting Mass Culture* (Minneapolis: University of Minnesota Press, 1993), 39–62.

39. "*Happy Days*," *Daily Variety*, 23 September 1976, 5, in USC clipping file for *Happy Days*.

40. McCrohan, *Prime Time*, 259; Grant Noble, "Social Learning from Everyday Television," in *Learning from Television: Psychological and Educational Research*, ed. Michael J. A. Howe (London: Academic Press, 1983), 109–11.

NOTES TO CHAPTER 5

1. A good statistical summary of the growth of VCRs and cables is readily available in *The Velvet Light Trap*, no. 27 (Spring 1991): 86–87. This variety does not necessarily imply diversity. On the conglomerate control of cable and media, see the "national entertainment state" issue of the *Nation* 262, no. 22 (3 June 1996). Also see Janet Wasko, *Hollywood in the Information Age: Beyond the Silver Screen* (Austin: University of Texas Press, 1994).

2. Mike Budd and Clay Steinman, "White Racism and 'The Cosby Show,'" *Jump Cut*, no. 37 (July 1992): 5. *The Simpsons* took away *Cosby*'s audience of children and younger males and it dropped to fifth

for 1990–91. *Roseanne* did tie *The Cosby Show* for number one in 1989–90 with both rated at 23.1, but *Roseanne* was not programmed opposite *The Cosby Show*. *The Cosby Show* might well have continued in the lower twenties if it had not faced the direct competition provided by *The Simpsons*.

3. NBC public relations material, 24 September 1984, in University of Southern California [hereafter USC] clipping file for *The Cosby Show*; Linda K. Fuller, *The Cosby Show: Audiences, Impact, and Implications* (Westport, Conn.: Greenwood Press, 1992), 20 and 41.

4. Critical analysis includes Budd and Steinman, "White Racism and 'The Cosby Show,'" 5–14; John D. H. Downing, "'The Cosby Show' and American Racial Discourse," in *Discourse and Discrimination*, ed. Geneva Smitherman-Donaldson and Teun A. van Dijk (Detroit, Mich.: Wayne State University Press, 1988), 46–73; John Fiske, *Media Matters: Everyday Culture and Political Change* (Minneapolis: University of Minnesota Press, 1994), 97–123; June M. Frazer and Timothy C. Frazer, "'Father Knows Best' and 'The Cosby Show': Nostalgia and the Sitcom Tradition," *Journal of Popular Culture* 27, no. 3 (Winter 1993): 163–72; Herman Gray, "Television and the New Black Man: Black Male Images in Prime Time Situation Comedy," *Media, Culture and Society* 8, no. 2 (1986): 223–42; Herman Gray, *Watching Race: Television and the Struggle for "Blackness"* (Minneapolis: University of Minnesota Press, 1995); Bishetta D. Merritt, "Billy Cosby: TV Auteur?" *Journal of Popular Culture* 24, no. 4 (Spring 1991): 89–102; Michael Real, "Bill Cosby and Recoding Ethnicity," in *Television Criticism: Approaches and Applications*, ed. Leah R. Vande Berg and Lawrence A. Wenner (New York: Longman, 1991), 58–84. Quantitative studies of audiences and possible effects are Venise T. Berry, "From *Good Times* to *The Cosby Show*: Perceptions of Changing Televised Images among Black Fathers and Sons," in *Men, Masculinity and the Media*, ed. Steve Craig (Newbury Park, Cal.: Sage Publications, 1992), 111–23; S. Fazal and W. Wober, *The Cosby Show: Some Black and White Audience Perceptions and Possibilities* (London: Independent Broadcasting Authority, November 1989); Fuller, *Cosby Show*; Leslie B. Inniss and Joe R. Feagin,

"*The Cosby Show*: The View from the Black Middle Class," *Journal of Black Studies* (Newbury Park, Cal.), 25, no. 6 (July 1995): 692–711; Sut Jhally and Justin Lewis, *Enlightened Racism: The Cosby Show, Audiences, and the Myth of the American Dream* (Boulder, Colo.: Westview Press, 1992); Justin Lewis, *The Ideological Octopus: An Exploration of Television and Its Audience* (New York: Routledge, 1991); Paula W. Matabane, "Television and the Black Audience: Cultivating Moderate Perspectives on Racial Integration," *Journal of Communication* 38, no. 4 (Autumn 1988): 21–31.

5. "Season Finally Begins to Jell As CBS-TV Picks Up on Monday; Tuesday a Powerhouse on NBC," *Variety*, 24 October 1984, 400; "NBC-TV Still Leads Season; CBS Is Gaining," *Variety*, 31 October 1984, 78.

6. Jack Loftus, "Webs Shares Falling, Sweeps No Help," *Variety*, 21 November 1984, 31; Bob Knight, "Year of the Sitcom for TV Nets: 'Cosby' Sets Precedent, ABC Hits on Tuesday," *Variety*, 4 December 1985, 1.

7. Ratings for period ending 25 May 1984, A. C. Nielsen Company, *Nielsen National TV Ratings* (A. C. Nielsen).

8. Leslie Bennetts, "Bill Cosby Begins Taping NBC Series," *New York Times*, 6 August 1984, sect 3, p. 20; "Carsey/Werner shoot 'Cosby' in New York," *Hollywood Reporter*, 20 August 1984, in USC clipping file for *The Cosby Show*.

9. John J. O'Connor, "Cosby in NBC Series on a New York Family," *New York Times*, 20 September 1984, sect. 3, p. 30.

10. John Leonard, "Leave It to Cosby," *New York*, 22 October 1984, 154.

11. Tom Carson, "Cosby Knows Best," *Village Voice* 29 (23 October 1984): 73. Not only echoing famous 1950s sitcoms in the titles of their articles, both Leonard and Carson contrast Cosby to Richard Pryor and Eddie Murphy (see below for Leonard's remarks).

12. Gray, "Television and the New Black Man," 227. Also see the caustic analysis of Mark Crispin Miller, "Prime Time: Deride and Conquer" in *Watching Television*, ed. Todd Gitlin (New York: Pantheon

Books, 1986), 183–228. Miller decries not only the white "lunatic fantasies of containment" of blacks (p. 213) but also the function of "neo-dads" as comic relief.

13. Thomas Cripps, "*Amos 'n' Andy* and the Debate over American Racial Integration," in *American History/American Television: Interpreting the Video Past*, ed. John E. O'Connor (New York: Ungar, 1983), 33–54.

14. Leonard, "Leave It to Cosby," 154.

15. Sally Bedell Smith, "Cosby Puts His Stamp on a TV Hit," *New York Times*, 19 November 1984, sect. 2, p. 1; Brian Winston, "Cosby's New Show: A Hit and a Myth," *Channels* 4, no. 5 (January–February 1985): 83; Lynn Norment, "*The Cosby Show*," *Ebony* 40 (April 1985): 27–30+; Robert Staples and Terry Jones, "Culture, Ideology and Black Television Images," *Black Scholar* 16, no. 2 (May/June 1985): 10–20.

16. O'Connor, "Cosby in NBC Series," p. 30; Leonard, "Leave It to Cosby," 154.

17. Carson, "Cosby Knows Best," 73.

18. Henry Jenkins, *What Made Pistachio Nuts? Early Sound Comedy and the Vaudeville Aesthetic* (New York: Columbia University Press, 1992), 26–58.

19. Although the audience preference was not to last. *The Simpsons* and *Roseanne* became the next wave of sitcom successes.

20. Bennetts, "Bill Cosby Begins Taping," p. 20.

21. Smith, "Cosby Puts His Stamp on a TV Hit," p. 1; Harry F. Waters, "Bill Cosby Comes Home," *Newsweek*, 5 November 1984, 93; Cathleen Schine, "A Good Cos," *Vogue* 175 (January 1985): 54.

22. Martha Bayles, "Lovable Huxtable's Bone-Deep Irony," *Wall Street Journal*, 19 November 1984, 30.

23. Kathleen Fury, "Witness the Humors of Bill Cosby," *TV Guide*, 13 October 1984, 35–36.

24. "Jitterbug Break," air date 31 January 1985; "Theo and the Joint," 7 February 1985; "Vanessa's New Class," 14 February 1985; "Clair's Case," 21 February 1985; "Back to the Track, Jack," 28 Feb-

ruary 1985; "The Younger Woman," 14 March 1985; "Slumber Party," 28 March 1985; and "Mr. Quiet," 2 May 1985.

25. This tradition and strategy goes back much further (into pretelevision and prefilm). These examples simply locate the method to closer texts.

26. A good counterexample is "Mr. Quiet," air date 2 May 1985, which is almost like a visit to Sesame Street. Cliff and Claire visit the local community center, but the narrative centers on a young boy who is in trouble.

27. Miller, "Prime Time," 209.

28. *Seinfeld* is jokingly considered to have been a show about nothing because a second-season episode had Jerry and George pitching such a program to NBC executives. *Seinfeld* is about nothing in that its characters' concerns about mores and manners are comparatively insignificant. However, in terms of plot construction, *Seinfeld* is one of the most elaborately designed sitcoms to have been on TV. Moreover, the plots habitually hinge around misunderstandings.

NOTES TO THE EPILOGUE

1. Hence, possibly, the complexity of identifications by audiences of this program as well as the opportunity to confront these issues more directly than in the other shows.

2. Early reviews of the program expected a more explicit representation of black culture, assuming, I think, that it should come in perhaps stereotyped terms: drugs, single mothers, and so forth. As the criticism rolled in, the program does seem to have responded to these observations, and this cultural distinction became more apparent in the plots after the first half of the first season. Still here is where textual analysis versus reception studies is important. Ultimately, I would argue, the fact that reviewers did not see this black culture as "there" is more important than my finding it in the plots and mise-en-scène.

3. Anita Gates, "This Fall, You Really Do Need a Scorecard," *New York Times*, 29 October 1995, H37.

4. Mike Peters, "Mother Goose and Grim," 6 October 1993; Mike Peters, "Mother Goose and Grim," 12 September 1993.

5. J. Fred MacDonald, *One Nation under Television: The Rise and Decline of Network TV* (Chicago, Ill.: Nelson-Hall Publishers, 1994), 202, 223–28; "Television," *Consumer Reports* September 1991, 576— data from A. C. Nielsen. Also see Janet Wasko, *Hollywood in the Information Age: Beyond the Silver Screen* (Austin: University of Texas Press, 1994), 113–70.

6. MacDonald, *One Nation under Television,* 228; "Television," 576; Peter Ainslie, "Confronting a Nation of Grazers," *Channels* 8, no. 8 (September 1988): 54.

7. Ainslie, "Confronting a Nation of Grazers," 54.

8. MacDonald, *One Nation under Television*, 249–52.

9. James Sterngold, "A Racial Divide Widens on Network TV," *New York Times*, 29 December 1998, 1.

Select Bibliography

A. C. Nielsen Company. *Nielsen National TV Ratings*. A. C. Nielsen.

Adler, Richard P., ed. *All in the Family: A Critical Appraisal*. New York: Praeger, 1979.

Adorno, Theodor W., and Max Horkheimer. "The Culture Industry: Enlightenment as Mass Deception" [1944]. In *The Dialectic of Enlightenment*, trans. John Cumming. New York: Herder and Herder, 1972. Pp. 120–67.

Anderson, Christopher. *Hollywood TV: The Studio System in the Fifties*. Austin: University of Texas Press, 1994.

Ang, Ien. *Desperately Seeking the Audience*. London: Routledge, 1991.

Attallah, Paul. "Situation Comedy and 'The Beverly Hillbillies': The Unworthy Discourse." Montreal, Quebec: Working Papers in Communication, McGill University, 1983.

Balio, Tino, ed. *Hollywood in the Age of Television*. Boston: Unwin Hyman, 1990.

Barnouw, Erik. *Tube of Plenty: The Evolution of American Television*. Rev. ed. Oxford: Oxford University Press, 1982.

Bedell, Sally. *Up the Tube: Prime-Time TV and the Silverman Years*. New York: Viking, 1981.

Bergreen, Lawrence. *Look Now, Pay Later: The Rise of Network Broadcasting*. New York: Doubleday and Co., 1980.

Berry, Venise T. "From *Good Times* to *The Cosby Show*: Perceptions of Changing Televised Images among Black Fathers and Sons." In *Men, Masculinity and the Media*, ed. Steve Craig. Newbury Park, Cal.: Sage Publications, 1992. Pp. 111–23.

Beville, Hugh Malcolm, Jr. *Audience Ratings: Radio, Television, and Cable*. Rev. ed. Hillsdale, N.J.: Lawrence Erlbaum Associates, 1988.

Boddy, William. "Building the World's Largest Advertising Medium: CBS and Television, 1940–60." In *Hollywood in the Age of Television*, ed. Balio. Pp. 63–89.

Bordwell, David, Janet Staiger, and Kristin Thompson. *The Classical Hollywood Cinema: Film Style and Mode of Production to 1960*. London: Routledge & Kegan Paul, 1985.

Brown, Les. *Televi$ion: The Business behind the Box*. New York: Harcourt Brace Jovanovich, 1971.

Bryant, John. "Emma, Lucy and the American Situation Comedy of Manners." *Journal of Popular Culture* 13, no. 2 (Fall 1979): 248–55.

Budd, Mike, and Clay Steinman. "White Racism and 'The Cosby Show.'" *Jump Cut*, no. 37 (July 1992): 5–14.

Butsch, Richard. "Class and Gender in Four Decades of Television Situation Comedy: Plus ça Change." *Critical Studies in Mass Communication* 9 (December 1992): 387–99.

Caldwell, John Thornton. *Televisuality: Style, Crisis, and Authority in American Television*. New Brunswick, N.J.: Rutgers University Press, 1995.

Cawelti, John G. "*Chinatown* and Generic Transformation in Recent American Films" [1979]. In *Film Theory and Criticism*, ed. Gerald Mast and Marshall Cohen. 3d ed. New York: Oxford University Press, 1985. Pp. 503–20.

Cook, Jim. "Narrative, Comedy Character and Performance." In *Television Sitcom*, ed. Cook. Pp. 13–18.

———, ed. *Television Sitcom*. BFI Dossier #17. London: British Film Institute, 1982.

Cox, Stephen. *The Beverly Hillbillies*. New York: HarperCollins Publishers, 1993.

Cripps, Thomas. "*Amos 'n' Andy* and the Debate over American Racial Integration." In *American History/American Television*, ed. O'Connor. Pp. 33–54.

Curtin, Michael. *Redeeming the Wasteland: Television Documentary and Cold War Politics*. New Brunswick, N.J.: Rutgers University Press, 1995.

Curtis, Barry. "Aspects of Sitcom." In *Television Sitcom*, ed. Cook. Pp. 4–12.

Dates, Jannette L., and William Barlow. *Split Image: African Americans in the Mass Media*. Washington, D.C.: Howard University Press, 1990.

Deeb, Gary. "The Man Who Destroyed Television." *Playboy* 26 (October 1979): 154–56+.

Deming, Robert. "*Kate and Allie*: 'New Women' and the Audiences' Television Archive." *camera obscura* 16 (January 1988): 154–76.

Doty, Alexander. *Making Things Perfectly Queer: Interpreting Mass Culture*. Minneapolis: University of Minnesota Press, 1993.

Downing, John D. H. "'The Cosby Show' and American Racial Discourse." In *Discourse and Discrimination*, ed. Geneva Smitherman-Donaldson and Teun A. van Dijk. Detroit, Mich.: Wayne State University Press, 1988. Pp. 46–73.

Eaton, Mick. "Laughter in the Dark." *Screen* 22, no. 2 (1981): 21–28.

———. "Television Situation Comedy." *Screen* 19, no. 4 (Winter 1978/79): 61–89.

Eisner, Joel, and David Krinsky. *Television Comedy Series: An Episode Guide to 153 TV Sitcoms in Syndication*. Jefferson, N.C.: McFarland & Company, 1984.

Fazal, S., and W. Wober. *The Cosby Show: Some Black and White Audience Perceptions and Possibilities*. London: Independent Broadcasting Authority, November 1989.

Feuer, Jane. "The MTM Enterprises: An Overview." In *MTM: "Quality Television,"* ed. Feuer, Kerr, and Vahimagi. Pp. 1–31.

———. "The MTM Style." In *MTM: "Quality Television,"* ed. Feuer, Kerr, and Vahimagi. Pp. 32–60.

Feuer, Jane, Paul Kerr, and Tise Vahimagi, eds. *MTM: "Quality Television."* London: British Film Institute, 1984.

Fishbein, Leslie. "*Roots*: Docudrama and the Interpretation of History." In *American History/American Television*, ed. O'Connor. Pp. 279–305.

Fiske, John. *Media Matters: Everyday Culture and Political Change.* Minneapolis: University of Minnesota Press, 1994.

————. *Television Culture.* London: Methuen, 1987.

Frazer, June M., and Timothy C. Frazer. "'Father Knows Best' and 'The Cosby Show': Nostalgia and the Sitcom Tradition." *Journal of Popular Culture* 27, no. 3 (Winter 1993): 163–74.

Freud, Sigmund. *Jokes and Their Relation to the Unconscious* [1905]. Trans. James Strachey. New York: W. W. Norton & Company, 1960.

Fuller, Linda K. *The Cosby Show: Audiences, Impact, and Implications.* Westport, Conn.: Greenwood Press, 1992.

Gitlin, Todd. *Inside Prime Time.* New York: Pantheon Books, 1983.

————, ed. *Watching Television.* New York: Pantheon Books, 1986.

Gladden, Jack. "Archie Bunker Meets Mr. Spoopendyke: Nineteenth-Century Prototypes for Domestic Situation Comedy." *Journal of Popular Culture* 10, no. 1 (Summer 1976): 167–80.

Gray, Herman. "Television and the New Black Man: Black Male Images in Prime Time Situation Comedy." *Media, Culture and Society* 8, no. 2 (1986): 223–42.

————. *Watching Race: Television and the Struggle for "Blackness."* Minneapolis: University of Minnesota Press, 1995.

Hamamoto, Darrell Y. *Nervous Laughter: Television Situation Comedy and Liberal Democratic Ideology.* New York: Praeger, 1989.

Haralovich, Mary Beth. "Sit-Coms and Suburbs: Positioning the 1950s Homemaker" [1988]. In *Private Screenings: Television and the Female Consumer,* ed. Lynn Spigel and Denise Mann. Minneapolis: University of Minnesota Press, 1992. Pp. 110–41.

Hilmes, Michele. *Hollywood and Broadcasting: From Radio to Cable.* Urbana: University of Illinois Press, 1990.

Hirsch, Paul M. "Processing Fads and Fashions: An Organization-Set Analysis of Cultural Industry Systems." *American Journal of Sociology* 77 (1972): 639–59. Rpt. in *Rethinking Popular Culture: Contemporary Perspectives in Cultural Studies,* ed. Chandra Mukerji and Michael Schudson. Berkeley: University of California Press, 1991. Pp. 313–34.

Horowitz, Susan. "Sitcom Domesticus—A Species Endangered by Social Change" [1984]. Rpt. in *Television*, ed. Newcomb. Pp. 106–11.

Inniss, Leslie B., and Joe R. Feagin. "*The Cosby Show*: The View from the Black Middle Class." *Journal of Black Studies* (Newbury Park, Cal.) 25, no. 6 (July 1995): 692–711.

Jameson, Fredric. "On Magic Realism in Film." *Critical Inquiry* 12, no. 2 (Winter 1986): 301–25.

Jenkins, Henry. *What Made Pistachio Nuts? Early Sound Comedy and the Vaudeville Aesthetic*. New York: Columbia University Press, 1992.

Jenkins, Henry, and Kristine Brunovska Karnick, eds. *Classical Hollywood Comedy*. New York: Routledge, 1995.

Jhally, Sut, and Justin Lewis. *Enlightened Racism: The Cosby Show, Audiences, and the Myth of the American Dream*. Boulder, Colo.: Westview Press, 1992.

Jones, Gerard. *Honey, I'm Home! Sitcoms: Selling the American Dream*. New York: Grove Weidenfeld, 1992.

Kaes, Anton. *From Hitler to Heimat: The Return of History as Film*. Cambridge: Harvard University Press, 1989.

Kerr, Paul. "The Making of (The) MTM (Show)." In *MTM: "Quality Television*," ed. Feuer, Kerr, and Vahimagi. Pp. 61–98.

Leibman, Nina C. "Leave Mother Out: The Fifties Family in American Film and Television." *Wide Angle* 10, no. 4 (1988): 24–41.

———. *Living Room Lectures: The Fifties Family in Film and Television*. Austin: University of Texas Press, 1995.

Lewis, Justin. *The Ideological Octopus: An Exploration of Television and Its Audience*. New York: Routledge, 1991.

Londoner, David J. "The Changing Economics of Entertainment" [1978/79]. In *The American Film Industry*, ed. Tino Balio. Rev. ed. Madison: University of Wisconsin Press, 1985. Pp. 603–30.

Lovell, Terry. "A Genre of Social Disruption?" In *Television Sitcom*, ed. Cook. Pp. 19–31.

MacDonald, J. Fred. *One Nation under Television: The Rise and Decline of Network TV.* Chicago, Ill.: Nelson-Hall Publishers, 1994.

Magoc, Chris J. "The Machine in the Wasteland: Progress, Pollution, and the Pastoral in Rural-Based Television, 1954–1971," *Journal of Popular Film and Television* 19, no. 1 (Spring 1991): 25–34.

Marc, David. *Comic Visions: Television Comedy and American Culture.* Boston: Unwin Hyman, 1989.

———. *Demographic Vistas: Television in American Culture.* Philadelphia: University of Pennsylvania Press, 1984.

Marchand, Roland. "Visions of Classlessness, Quests for Dominion: American Popular Culture, 1945–1960." In *Reshaping America: Society and Institutions: 1945–1960*, ed. Robert H. Bremner and Gary W. Reichard. Columbus: Ohio State University Press, 1982. Pp. 163–90.

Marshall, Garry. *Wake Me When It's Funny: How to Break into Show Business and Stay There.* Holbrook, Mass.: Adams Publishing, 1995.

Matabane, Paula W. "Television and the Black Audience: Cultivating Moderate Perspectives on Racial Integration." *Journal of Communication* 38, no. 4 (Autumn 1988): 21–31.

McCrohan, Donna. *Archie and Edith, Mike and Gloria: The Tumultuous History of "All in the Family."* New York: Workman Publishing, 1987.

———. *Prime Time, Our Time: America's Life and Times through the Prism of Television.* Rocklin, Cal.: Prima Publishing & Communications, 1990.

Meehan, Eileen R. "Why We Don't Count: The Commodity Audience." In *Logics of Television: Essays in Cultural Criticism*, ed. Patricia Mellencamp. London: British Film Institute, 1990. Pp. 117–37.

Mellencamp, Patricia. "Situation and Simulation: An Introduction to 'I Love Lucy.'" *Screen* 26, no. 2 (March–April 1985): 30–40.

Merritt, Bishetta D. "Billy Cosby: TV Auteur?" *Journal of Popular Culture* 24, no. 4 (Spring 1991): 89–102.

Metz, Robert. *CBS: Reflections in a Bloodshot Eye.* New York: Playboy Press, 1975.

Miller, Mark Crispin. "Prime Time: Deride and Conquer" [1986]. In *Watching Television,* ed. Gitlin. Pp. 183–228.

Minow, Newton N. *Equal Time: The Private Broadcaster and the Public Interest.* New York: Athenaeum, 1964.

Monaco, James. *American Film Now: The People, the Power, the Money, the Movies.* New York: New American Library, 1979.

Newcomb, Horace, ed. *Television: The Critical View.* 4th ed. New York: Oxford University Press, 1987.

———. *TV: The Most Popular Art.* Garden City, N.Y.: Anchor Books, 1974.

Noble, Grant. "Social Learning from Everyday Television." In *Learning from Television: Psychological and Educational Research,* ed. Michael J. A. Howe. London: Academic Press, 1983. Pp. 101–24.

Norback, Craig T., and Peter G. Norback, eds. *TV Guide Almanac.* New York: Ballantine Books, 1980.

O'Connor, John E., ed. *American History/American Television: Interpreting the Video Past.* New York: Ungar, 1983.

Powell, Chris, and George E. C. Paton. Introduction. In *Humor in Society: Resistance and Control,* ed. Powell and Paton. London: Macmillan, 1988. Pp. xiii–xxi.

Rabinovitz, Lauren. "Sitcoms and Single Moms: Representations of Feminism on American TV." *Cinema Journal* 29, no. 1 (Fall 1989): 3–19.

Real, Michael. "Bill Cosby and Recoding Ethnicity." In *Television Criticism: Approaches and Applications,* ed. Leah R. Vande Berg and Lawrence A. Wenner. New York: Longman, 1991. Pp. 58–84.

Ross, Andrew. *No Respect: Intellectuals and Popular Culture.* New York: Routledge, 1989.

Sklar, Robert. *Prime-Time America: Life on and behind the Television Screen.* New York: Oxford University Press, 1980.

Spangler, Lynn C. "A Historical Overview of Female Friendships on Prime-Time Television." *Journal of Popular Culture* 22, no. 4 (Spring 1989): 13–25.

Spigel, Lynn. "From Domestic Space to Outer Space: The 1960s Fantastic Family Sit-Com." In *Close Encounters: Film, Feminism, and Science Fiction,* ed. Constance Penley, Elisabeth Lyon, Lynn Spigel, and Janet Bergstrom. Minneapolis: University of Minnesota Press, 1991. Pp. 205–35.

Staiger, Janet. "Hybrid or Inbred: The Purity Hypothesis and Hollywood Genre History." *Film Criticism* 22, no. 1 (Fall 1997): 5–20.

———. *Interpreting Films: Studies in the Historical Reception of American Cinema.* Princeton, N.J.: Princeton University Press, 1992.

Staples, Robert, and Terry Jones. "Culture, Ideology and Black Television Images." *Black Scholar* 16, no. 2 (May/June 1985): 10–20.

Steiner, Gary A. *The People Look at Television: A Study of Audience Attitudes.* New York: Alfred A. Knopf, 1963.

Sterling, Christopher H., and John M. Kittross. *Stay Tuned: A Concise History of American Broadcasting.* Belmont, Cal.: Wadsworth Publishing Company, 1978.

Taylor, Ella. *Prime-Time Families: Television Culture in Postwar America.* Berkeley: University of California Press, 1989.

Waldron, Vince. *Classic Sitcoms: A Celebration of the Best Prime-Time Comedy.* New York: Macmillan, 1987.

Wasko, Janet. *Hollywood in the Information Age: Beyond the Silver Screen.* Austin: University of Texas Press, 1994.

Watson, Mary Ann. "[From *My Little Margie* to *Murphy Brown*:] Images of Women [on Television]." *Television Quarterly* 27, no. 2 (1994): 4–24.

Wertheim, Arthur Frank. *Radio Comedy*. New York: Oxford University Press, 1979.

White, Mimi. "What's the Difference: *Frank's Place* in Television." *Wide Angle* 13, nos. 3/4 (1991): 82–93.

Index

About the Author

Janet Staiger is William P. Hobby Centennial Professor of Communication in the Department of Radio-Television-Film at the University of Texas at Austin. Her books include the landmark study *Interpreting Films: Studies in the Historical Reception of American Cinema* as well as *Bad Women: Regulating Sexuality in Early American Cinema, The Classical Hollywood Cinema* (with David Bordwell and Kristin Thompson), and *Perverse Spectators: The Practices of Film Reception* (also available from NYU Press).